PRAISE FOR
THE SMART
ADVERTISING BOOK

"With *The Smart Advertising Book* Dan White has created
an excellent compendium covering all aspects of
advertising best practice."

Nigel Hollis, Former Chief Global Brand Analyst, Kantar

"It's great – Dan's best yet!"

Mark Wieczorek, CTO Fortress Brand, New York

"A useful romp through the advertising ecosystem, with loads
of practical advice supported by proof points. It's both a primer
for those new to the industry and a reminder to those who
have worked in it for decades."

Karl Weaver, SVP, Head of Consulting EMEA, MediaLink

"Dan manages to communicate more in one illustration than some
learned commentators manage in several pages. His books are
a godsend for those of us with butterfly minds, as well as providing
our more thoughtful and disciplined colleagues with a beautifully
simple summation of what are often complicated theories."

Brian Jacobs, Founder, BJ&A

"Leave it to Dan to bring to life in the only way he can, all the current thinking and methodologies for today's advertising landscape. A great addition to his ever-growing library of great marketing books."

Vassilis K. Douros, Head of Digital Marketing, TELUS Consumer Solutions

"*The Smart Advertising Book* could arguably be Dan's greatest book so far. It provides a complete compendium of case studies, examples, frameworks, figures, historical data and factoids. Dan distils all subjects expertly and presents his ideas in an easy to comprehend style and format."

Gareth Walters, Director of International Operations, Europe, Middle East and Africa, Focus Brands International

"Dan's powerfully simple way of illustrating complex ideas takes a lot of the stress out of marketing."

Johnny Corbett, Chief Marketing and Revenues Officer, KinectAir

"Your trilogy of books should be recommended reading for all brand managers!"

Steve Messenger, CEO, RedRoute International Ltd

"Dan's broad view of an advertising model including long- and short-term effects is a great summary of some of the best of recent thinking."

Adrian Langford, Director of Strategy and Planning, Jaywing

"Not recommended for people who prefer long words and long-winded explanations."

Ethan Decker, Founder and President, Applied Brand Science

"Every entrepreneur and marketer needs *The Smart Advertising Book*. It's packed with actionable insights on every page."

Gabriel I. Agüero, Founding Partner, Drop Music Branding

"*The Smart Advertising Book* is a distilled manual that breaks away from bad, cookie-cutter guru advice to explain how brands actually grow. It's a fun, digestible read that should be frequently revisited as a reference guide."

Phillip Oakley, Founder, Common Giant

"I read Sharp, Romaniuk and Nelson-Field but when I want other people to understand what they are on about, I show them Dan's book. It gives you what you need, based on real-world research from the likes of the Ehrenberg-Bass Institute, WARC and the IPA."

Cris Ferguson, Chief Commercial Officer, ONNA

"There are few in advertising with the breadth of insight and razor-sharp clarity that Dan has. For those new to the industry and veterans, Dan's book makes essential reading."

Omaid Hiwaizi, Cofounder, Infinity Maritime

Published by
LID Publishing
An imprint of LID Business Media Ltd.
LABS House, 15-19 Bloomsbury Way,
London, WC1A 2TH, UK

info@lidpublishing.com
www.lidpublishing.com

A member of:

businesspublishersroundtable.com

All rights reserved. Without limiting the rights under copyright reserved,
no part of this publication may be reproduced, stored or introduced into
a retrieval system, or transmitted, in any form or by any means (electronic,
mechanical, photocopying, recording or otherwise) without the prior written
permission of both the copyright owners and the publisher of this book.

© Dan White, 2024
© LID Business Media Limited, 2024

Printed by Pelikan Basım

ISBN: 978-1-915951-18-2
ISBN: 978-1-915951-19-9 (ebook)

Cover and page design: Caroline Li

THE SMART ADVERTISING BOOK

HOW TO DELIVER ADVERTISING THAT GROWS YOUR BRAND

DAN WHITE

MADRID | MEXICO CITY | LONDON
BUENOS AIRES | BOGOTA | SHANGHAI

FOR OTHER TITLES
IN THE SERIES...

CONCISE
ADVICE
LAB

SMALL BOOKS: BIG IDEAS

CLEVER CONTENT, DYNAMIC IDEAS, PRACTICAL
SOLUTIONS AND ENGAGING VISUALS –
A CATALYST TO INSPIRE NEW WAYS OF THINKING
AND PROBLEM-SOLVING IN A COMPLEX WORLD

www.lidpublishing.com/product-category/concise-advice-series

CONTENTS

INTRODUCTION

Advertising can play many roles in business success. It can accelerate and amplify the sales growth of brands with strong products. It can make people feel that a brand is a good choice even if it doesn't have a significant product advantage. It can even increase the chances that your brand's future products will sell.

The catch is that developing advertising is difficult and involves a degree of risk for your business. Many brands invest time and money on advertising that has virtually no impact. Successful advertising requires collaboration across multiple business functions and external agencies. It must allow creativity to flourish while ensuring it is harnessed for the good of the brand. It demands the use of analytics to optimize content and choose the right media.

The Smart Advertising Book is a field guide for anyone involved in advertising development. It will help you navigate the process and provide your best chance of delivering world class advertising that drives commercial success. The nine chapters cover all aspects of advertising from basic principles to the latest thinking and best practices. You can dive straight to a section that's relevant to you now, but beginners are advised to read the book from start to finish.

- Chapter 1 explains the origins of advertising and the role it plays in the modern marketing mix
- Chapters 2, 3 & 4 explore the diverse media opportunities a brand can choose from
- Chapters 5 & 6 highlight different creative approaches a brand might take, depending on its communication priorities
- Chapters 7 & 8 are deep dives into developing effective static visual and video ads
- Chapter 9 outlines the market research techniques you can use to help identify effective advertising concepts, develop strong storylines, optimize final executions and measure campaign impact

Advertising is one of the most powerful levers for brand building. It works alongside naming, pricing, innovating, expanding and measuring your brand. You can learn more about how to combine these levers to create a profitable, resilient brand in *The Smart Branding Book*. Brand-building is part of a wider marketing mix that brand owners need to manage in order to drive long-term growth. *The Smart Marketing Book* guides you on how to do this. *The Smart Advertising Book* completes the trilogy, providing a deep dive into advertising, covering how to harness creativity and media to deliver exceptional business results.

THE
PURPOSE OF
ADVERTISING

1.1 THE ORIGINS OF ADVERTISING

The earliest forms of advertising can be traced back to ancient Egypt, where merchants used papyrus wall posters to promote their wares. Their posters typically presented simple slogans or statements, such as 'The best wine in town' or 'Buy our bread, it's the freshest in the market.' The oldest example is this flyer from a fabric seller named Hapu, dating from 3000 B.C., found in the ruins of Thebes. It requests that people track down a missing slave and bring him to Hapu's shop in return for a reward and the chance to sample the fine fabrics available there.

THE FIRST EVER AD

The ancient Greeks and Romans also used advertising to promote their businesses, with merchants putting signs above their shops or market stalls to indicate the goods they sold.

The modern concept of advertising began to take shape during the Industrial Revolution in the 18th and 19th centuries. With the rise of mass production and consumerism, businesses saw the opportunity to enhance growth through advertising. By the early 20th century, it was cost effective for brands to produce colourful and eye-catching advertisements for a mass audience. These were placed in popular newspapers and periodicals. This led to the growth of advertising agencies, companies that would create and place ads on behalf of their clients. Today, advertising is a complex and multifaceted industry, encompassing an ever-increasing range of media. *The Smart Advertising Book* will help you navigate this dynamic world, helping you to choose the right combination of media and leverage it for maximum commercial impact.

1.2 ROLES ADVERTISING CAN PLAY

The purpose of advertising remains the same as it was in ancient Egypt. Successful marketing plays two major roles.

BRAND BUILDING

This is designed to create an ongoing stream of future customers. Advertising can do this by establishing long-lasting memories in the minds of a broad range of potential customers. These memories mean that the brand and what it offers are more likely to come to people's minds, and feel relevant, whenever people think of buying the category. To achieve this, advertising needs to be noticed and remembered. A brand can be thought of as the set of associations connected with the brand's name that have built up in consumers' memories. Brand managers go to a lot of trouble when determining which associations would make the brand a compelling choice. Advertising plays a major role in building the desired set of mental associations (see Section 1.3 for more details).

THE ROLE OF ADVERTISING IN BRAND BUILDING

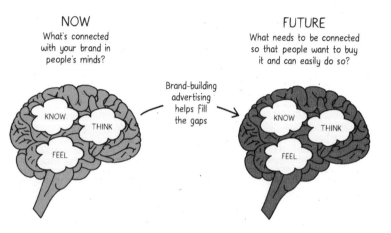

NOW
What's connected
with your brand in
people's minds?

FUTURE
What needs to be connected
so that people want to buy
it and can easily do so?

KNOW
THINK
FEEL

Brand-building
advertising
helps fill
the gaps

KNOW
THINK
FEEL

ACTIVATION

Most people have busy lives. If we spent too much time deciding which brands to buy, we'd have no time left for the things we care about. This explains why people make most purchase decisions without much thought. Having relevant and compelling brand associations is not always enough to drive sales. To influence purchasing, these associations need to come to consumers' minds when they are deciding what to buy.

This is where advertising designed to activate brand memories comes in. It reminds people of the brand and brings associations to mind when people are about to buy the category. It can also point people to where they could learn more about the brand or buy it.

HOW BRAND BUILDING AND ACTIVATION WORK TOGETHER

1.3 HOW ADVERTISING BUILDS BRANDS

Advertising can make a brand feel like a good choice by building a rich set of mental associations around it. This happens in three ways.

HOW ADVERTISING BUILDS BRANDS

FAMILIARITY

The primary task of advertising is to make people familiar with the brand and what it does. People favour things they have encountered before. This is a psychological phenomenon called the Mere Exposure Effect. Also, if a brand comes quickly to someone's mind when they think about buying the category, the brand has a better chance of being chosen. This is due to the psychological process known as Cognitive Ease – our tendency to make decisions quickly, based on instinctive thoughts rather than deliberation.

FIT

Over time, advertising can establish a strong fit between the brand and what people are looking for when buying the category. It does this by creating mental connections around the brand. If the associations are relevant to the consumer's decision, they help the brand spring to mind when people are thinking about their purchase, increasing the brand's chances of being chosen. These associations have an effect whenever the brand is brought to consumers' attention.

This is why marketing activity close to point of sale is effective. When people are thinking about which supermarket to visit, the Lidl brand may spring to mind along with the idea that they're 'always Lidl on price.' This makes Lidl feel like a good option, especially if the household budget is tight. When someone is thinking of buying a new car and they're looking for one that's well engineered and great to drive, BMW may be the first brand that comes to mind, thanks to the associations the brand has built up through advertising over the past few decades. Their tagline 'The Ultimate Driving Machine' helps people think of the brand if they're looking for a car they'll enjoy driving.

FAME

Advertising creates exceptional value if it makes the brand famous. Advertising that captures the public's imagination and becomes part of the culture can ensure the brand remains familiar and relevant for years or even decades to come. Advertising for insurance comparison website Comparethemarket.com catapulted the brand to fame in the UK and helped it become market leader almost overnight. The campaign featured charismatic, animated meerkats trying to iron out any confusion with their dating website 'Comparethemeerkat.com.' Fame can be very powerful. Although people don't like to admit it, they usually prefer to buy whatever they think other people are buying. This is due to a powerful psychological phenomenon referred to as Social Proof.

1.4 HOW ADVERTISING TRIGGERS PURCHASING

When a brand has strong mental connections, these can be activated by advertising at just the right time to influence consumers' purchase decision. Activation advertising includes:

- posters outside supermarkets that remind people of why they might want to buy a brand
- sponsored search results that direct people to the brand's website
- ads at sporting events that prompt attendees to buy a brand for a mid-game refreshment

Uber's 'Get a Ride' campaign in 2014 is a great illustration of the power of activation advertising. The campaign included TV to generate awareness and interest in Uber's service by highlighting its speed, convenience and reliability. Uber then activated this interest via billboard and mobile ads, which people saw when they were on the street waiting for a taxi or about to take the subway.

UBER ACTIVATION AD 2014

The campaign was highly successful and was credited with helping to drive the company's explosive growth.

THE COMMERCIAL VALUE OF ADVERTISING

If your brand delivers a strong user experience at an appropriate price, advertising is more likely to be a good investment. Promoting a sub-standard product, however, is a guaranteed waste of money. Advertising is a good investment if the increase in profit it generates is greater than its cost. The effects of advertising can span years, so its value greatly depends on whether your business has a short- or long-term focus.

Marketers can use several different statistics to measure return on investment (ROI) from their advertising. Be sure to use the most appropriate metric for making different marketing decisions. When discussing the topic with your colleagues and partners, clarify which ROI definition is being used.

REVENUE ROI

This is also known as Return on Advertising Spend (ROAS). It is calculated as follows:

$$\frac{\text{Additional sales generated by the advertising}}{\text{Media spend}}$$

For example, if media spending of £100k results in £220k additional sales, the Revenue ROI is said to be £220k/£100k = 2.2. In other words, the extra sales generated are more than twice the cost of the advertising. This sounds good, but don't be fooled – Revenue ROI can be misleading. In this example, if you make a 40% profit margin on your sales, the financial benefit from the advertising would be £220k X 40% which is just £88k, less than the £100k cost of the media. Be very careful when interpreting Revenue ROI. If your brand makes 20% profit on sales, a Revenue ROI of 5 would mean you only just break even (or worse, once you factor in the cost of producing the creative). Revenue ROI is fine for comparing the merits of different media channels, but it doesn't tell you if the advertising was a good or bad investment.

PROFIT ROI
Profit ROI is calculated as follows:

$$\frac{\text{Additional } \underline{\text{profit}} \text{ generated by the advertising}}{\text{Media spend}}$$

For example, if media spending of £200k results in £220k additional profit, the Profit ROI is said to be £220k/£200k = 1.1. Counterintuitively, this ROI may also be referred to as 10% – i.e., the extra profit generated by the advertising is 10% more than the cost of the media. Profit ROI provides a more accurate picture of whether the advertising is worth the investment, but the time and cost of producing the creative assets should also be factored in.

Revenue and Profit ROI can be estimated using econometric models. These compare the timing and levels of advertising expenditure to fluctuations in brand sales to estimate the advertising return. To isolate the impact of advertising they control for other factors affecting sales such as pricing, competitor activity and seasonality. Different modelling companies quote slightly different figures for the Profit ROI brands typically achieve, ranging between 5–10%. In other words, for every £1 spent on advertising, brand owners can expect an average profit uplift of between £1.05 and £1.10.

ROIs vary hugely by country, category and brand. The ROI your brand might achieve will depend on:

BRAND SIZE
Advertising spend tends to provide an uplift in sales that's proportionate to the brand's size. This means that big brands are bound to achieve a greater ROI than small brands.

AVAILABILITY
Great advertising can build demand, but if your brand isn't easily available, consumers will go elsewhere, and your advertising investment will be wasted. Brands with better distribution achieve a higher ROI.

USER EXPERIENCE
If your brand delivers a good user experience for the price, you are likely to enjoy high levels of repeat purchase. This means that the money you spend on advertising to attract new customers is a good investment.

CREATIVE QUALITY

Advertising ROI varies enormously depending on the quality of the creative. Kantar's database of over 1,000 US online video advertisements highlights the variation. The graph shows how the uplift in advertisement awareness from the same number of impressions can be as little as 1% or over 10%, depending on the creative.

The difference in profit returns between below and above average creative quality is considerable.

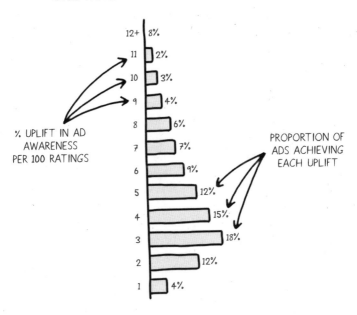

CREATIVE IMPACT VARIES HUGELY

12+	8%
11	2%
10	3%
9	4%
8	6%
7	7%
6	9%
5	12%
4	15%
3	18%
2	12%
1	4%

% UPLIFT IN AD AWARENESS PER 100 RATINGS

PROPORTION OF ADS ACHIEVING EACH UPLIFT

Kantar partnered with the World Advertising Research Centre to quantify the benefit of creative quality. They compared pre-test results with returns measured by market mix modelling and found that above-average creative delivered a return nearly five times greater than below-average creative.

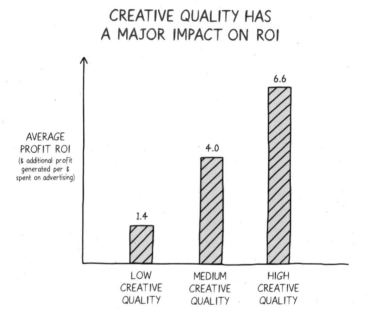

CREATIVE QUALITY HAS
A MAJOR IMPACT ON ROI

AVERAGE PROFIT ROI
($ additional profit generated per $ spent on advertising)

6.6

4.0

1.4

LOW CREATIVE QUALITY

MEDIUM CREATIVE QUALITY

HIGH CREATIVE QUALITY

TIMEFRAME

Truly exceptional advertising can be remembered and continue to elevate sales for decades. According to Dyson and Weaver (2006), you need to evaluate advertising by considering both the short and long term. The long-term effect (approx. 2-3 years) is typically three to five times bigger than the short-term effect (approx. 3-6 months).

LONG-TERM AD EFFECTS
OUTWEIGH SHORT-TERM

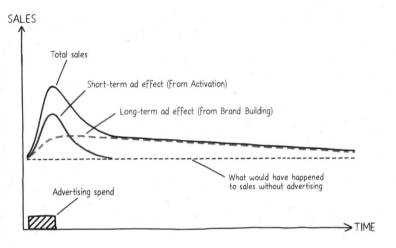

Some advertising campaigns provide good ROI thanks to the short-term effect alone. Even campaigns that don't pay back in the short term might still be a good investment if the long-term effect is large enough. The challenge for marketers is that it usually takes 12 months or more before the long-term effect can be measured accurately, even with the most sophisticated econometric modelling. The decision about whether to continue investing in a campaign may need to be made before the supporting sales data is available. If so, copy test and brand tracking data can be used to guide the decision in the meantime (see Chapter 9).

CHAPTER 2

MEDIA STRATEGY

2.1 SETTING YOUR MEDIA BUDGET

Developing advertising requires significant management time and production costs. When deciding how much to spend on advertising, you need to ask yourself how much will be used producing the creative and how much will be left for media. Your return from media needs to cover the cost of production and deliver a profit beyond it. This can be challenging, especially for brands with low spending power.

As you increase your media spend, you will also start to see diminishing returns. The first time someone sees your advertising, the impact on them is large. The next few exposures also have a strong incremental effect but the difference between seeing the advertising 10 versus 11 times, for example, is small. The effect is worse if the exposures are all to the same or a similar ad, in the same media channel, or within a short space of time.

AD EXPOSURES PROVIDE DIMINISHING RETURNS

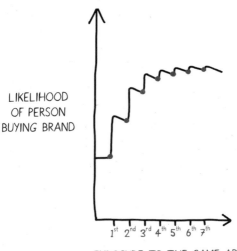

LIKELIHOOD OF PERSON BUYING BRAND

1ˢᵗ 2ⁿᵈ 3ʳᵈ 4ᵗʰ 5ᵗʰ 6ᵗʰ 7ᵗʰ

EXPOSURE TO THE SAME AD

Given that diminishing returns are unavoidable, you might expect that the efficiency of a brand's advertising as they invest more would decrease. However, this is not entirely true.

Academic and industry research indicates there is a sweet spot for advertising spend. Sales modelling specialist Magic Numbers (Magicnumbers.co.uk, 2023) have found that businesses spending 5-10% of their revenues on media achieve maximum ROI.

HOW MUCH TO INVEST IN ADVERTISING

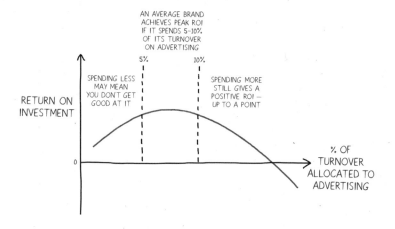

One reason that efficiency initially increases may be that the quality of advertising improves as a business devotes more time and money to it. It gains access to more talented creative teams, uses more channels, and obtains better media advice and deals. Peak ROI occurs at a higher percentage of turnover if you have a small brand, brilliant creative, or sell at a high profit margin.

Of course, the advertising may continue to deliver excellent ROI at much higher levels of spend. In fact, some brands will need to spend more to remain competitive, depending on how much other brands are spending. According to Binet and Field (2016), to hold their position, brands need their share of spend to be roughly in line with their share of the market (by value). Also, if they have the available funding, brands may decide to invest well above the optimum range in order to establish dominance in a category.

2.2 CHOOSING YOUR MEDIA

There is a bewildering array of different media types to choose from. These include media that you pay for, media that you own, and earned media you have little control over. Earned media include what people say about your brand face to face, in traditional and social media, or via product reviews and ratings.

PAID, OWNED AND EARNED MEDIA

PAID   OWNED   EARNED

If used creatively, most media can be used for any advertising task. However, some are better suited to certain jobs. In the illustration below, media are placed nearer to the job(s) they are often used for.

ROLES THAT DIFFERENT MEDIA OFTEN PLAY

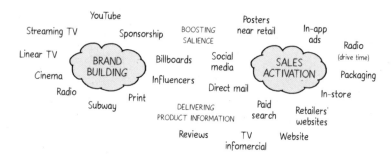

Cinema and TV, for example, are particularly good for creating long-lasting memories that build the brand. This is because they are audio-visual and hold people's attention for longer than other media (provided the creative is engaging enough – see Section 2.3). Infomercials, print and influencers are good for when people need more explanation to appreciate why they should consider buying your brand.

To trigger purchasing, you need to use media that people are exposed to close to the decision moment. This varies significantly by category. For brands that are bought online, paid search and retailer websites/apps work well. For brands bought on the high street, city centre posters and in-store advertising are ideal.

There are five things you need to consider when choosing which media channels to use.

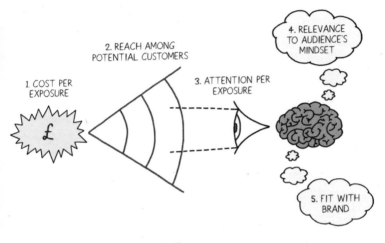

WHAT TO CONSIDER WHEN CHOOSING MEDIA CHANNELS

2. REACH AMONG POTENTIAL CUSTOMERS

4. RELEVANCE TO AUDIENCE'S MINDSET

1. COST PER EXPOSURE

£

3. ATTENTION PER EXPOSURE

5. FIT WITH BRAND

COST PER EXPOSURE
To ensure you are getting good value for money, prioritize channels that reach your potential customers at a reasonable cost. You can use well-established industry datasets, such as Kantar's Target Group Index (TGI), to estimate the reach of most major media channels.

REACH AMONG POTENTIAL CUSTOMERS
Niche channels can offer great value, but they might not reach a significant proportion of your target audience. Channel reach is an important consideration because attracting new and lapsed users is key to achieving brand growth (see Section 2.6).

ATTENTION PER EXPOSURE

Next, bear in mind how much attention people are likely to pay to your advertising, given how they use the medium. Research from the eye-tracking company Lumen (Dentsu.com, 2021) shows that the amount of time people spend looking at advertising varies a lot by medium.

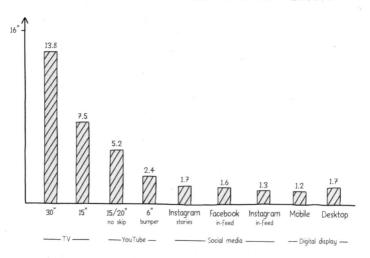

AVERAGE EYES-ON DWELL TIME BY MEDIUM

These differences are important because the longer people spend watching an ad, the more likely they are to remember it. A study commissioned by media company Dentsu (2021) shows that advertisements watched for 2 seconds increase brand choice by 5%, on average, whereas advertisements watched for 14 seconds increase brand choice by 9%. Levels of attention should be factored in, alongside reach and cost, when deciding which media channels to use.

RELEVANCE TO AUDIENCE'S MINDSET

People are more likely to pay attention to advertising if it is relevant to their current needs or desires. For example, as young, urban professionals emerge from the subway after work, they often think about the evening ahead. This is an ideal moment to advertise a low alcohol beer.

CONSIDER MINDSET WHEN CHOOSING MEDIA

Technology can now enable ads to be served to people for whom the message is highly relevant at that moment. For example, ads for train services can be delivered to drivers who have just had a difficult journey to work, ads for waterproof jackets to people caught outdoors in the rain and ads for home security systems to people who have just watched the news.

FIT WITH BRAND

The final consideration is how people's perceptions of your brand might be affected by advertising in a particular channel. How would people's opinion of Gucci products be affected if they were sold in the 'grab a bargain' middle aisle of ALDI stores? As Sancho Panza says in *Don Quixote*, "Tell me the company you keep, and I will tell you who you are." The media you choose to advertise your brand tells people a lot about your brand, regardless of your explicit messaging.

Once you have identified a set of channels that are relevant to your brand's objectives, you need to decide which combination to use. Snyder and Garcia-Garcia (2016) showed that using multiple channels is more effective than putting all your eggs into one basket. You should always aim for your campaign to include elements designed to build the brand and elements designed to activate purchase (see Section 2.4). To maximize your return from advertising investment, it is worth commissioning a media agency and seeking advice from a media planning expert (see Section 2.3).

2.3 PARTNERING COMMUNICATIONS AGENCIES

Devising, producing and deploying advertising requires specialist skills. Even the world's largest advertisers usually outsource creative development, media planning and media. Some agencies offer a full service, but if you plan to use a variety of media, you'll probably need to work with multiple media and creative partners. To achieve good results, choose the right partners and work with them in a productive way.

CHOOSING YOUR AGENCY PARTNER(S)

Look for agencies with a good track record with brands like yours. Ask to see case studies of successful partnerships with brands of a similar size, in similar categories, with similar marketing challenges and budgets, and using the kinds of channel you're likely to use (see Section 2.2). Talk to the individuals who would be working with you day-to-day. Make sure you'd find them easy to work with and that they are keen to work with you. Check they have a broadly similar view on the role advertising should play in the success of your brand.

Activities in different media channels need to work well together, connect with each other, and be sequenced to maximize their effectiveness. You should appoint a lead media agency with the responsibility of coordinating the activities of other agency partners, such as specialists in a particular medium. Similarly, identify a lead creative agency that will develop a creative vision for your brand, and work to ensure all content agencies stay true to this vision. This is essential for building a strong, coherent brand identity. The roles and responsibilities of media and creative agencies are often blurred, so you will need to spend time clarifying who does what at the beginning of the partnership.

COLLABORATING WITH YOUR AGENCIES

Once you have chosen your agency partners, treat them as if they were part of your organization. Be open to their ideas and encourage them to be bold and creative in their recommendations. To ensure effective communications, identify a single point of contact within your organization who will obtain and reconcile feedback from different business stakeholders and guide the agency accordingly. To establish a strong working relationship and avoid last-minute changes, it's worth scheduling regular check-ins. This will help to identify any issues in time to resolve them.

When working with an agency for the first time, provide them with a thorough briefing on your business. Think of ways to help them understand how consumers think about the category and your brand. Consider involving consumers in the briefing and providing ways for your partners to experience the product or service. Give a product demonstration and allow the agency team to sample the product. Goodie bags are always popular. Retail visits can also be valuable. The more contextual information you provide, the better. Be open about your company's goals, how you see the competition and what you think needs to be done for your brand to come out on top.

HOW TO BRIEF YOUR
COMMUNICATIONS AGENCIES

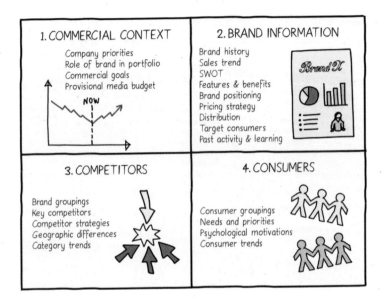

1. COMMERCIAL CONTEXT	2. BRAND INFORMATION
Company priorities Role of brand in portfolio Commercial goals Provisional media budget	Brand history Sales trend SWOT Features & benefits Brand positioning Pricing strategy Distribution Target consumers Past activity & learning
3. COMPETITORS	4. CONSUMERS
Brand groupings Key competitors Competitor strategies Geographic differences Category trends	Consumer groupings Needs and priorities Psychological motivations Consumer trends

If you provide your agencies with all this information, they will be well equipped to offer high quality recommendations for all aspects of your advertising.

WORKING ON A SPECIFIC COMMUNICATIONS PROJECT

A successful communications project starts with an effective brief. Use the template below to make sure you have thought things through. Involve trusted individuals from your agencies to help you develop the brief. When it's ready, bring your media and creative teams together if you can, ideally face to face, to foster a spirit of collaboration and ensure everyone is on the same page. The agencies may ask you to adopt their own templates when briefing them. If so, make sure the information described in the template is passed on during the briefing process.

COMMUNICATIONS PROJECT BRIEF TEMPLATE

In addition to timeframes and a ballpark budget, the brief should include the following...

Describe the target audience. What lifestyle do they lead? What are their priorities?	What insight, that resonates with consumers, should all the communications relate back to?	What needs/desires does the brand fulfil? How do these connect to the insight?
What else should we know about the brand and its competitive situation?	Which associations & feelings should the communications evoke?	Which specific visuals, sounds, words/phrases/ personalities/characters must be featured?
Which consumer behaviours should be affected? Immediate action? General increase in purchase likelihood?	Which commercial KPIs are we aiming to change? By how much? By when?	Please illustrate how the idea could come alive across multiple touchpoints including...

After a few weeks, your lead media agency should provide their point of view on:

- Specific media to use and how they will work together
- Allocation of budget to each medium
- Timing of each campaign element
- Evaluation metrics and targets

Your lead creative agency should provide their suggestions for:

- The brand idea* (if a new one is needed)
- The creative idea*
- How the campaign could be brought to life using diverse media formats
- Descriptions or rough prototypes for possible executions in the recommended media

(*See section 5.1)

GETTING THE MOST FROM YOUR CREATIVE PARTNERS

If you want a good return from your media investment, you'll need your agencies to produce highly creative, original work. Creative quality has a huge influence on advertising effectiveness, arguably more than factors such as media reach or targeting. It's sometimes referred to as 'the most variable of variables' when it comes to media ROI. According to marketing effectiveness experts Nielsen (2017), the quality of creative work determines nearly 50% of advertising effectiveness.

Creativity is important because advertising that's different, unexpected and emotionally resonant is better able to bypass people's attention filter. This means it either gets noticed and acted upon immediately or it sinks into memory to affect purchase decisions weeks, months and even years later.

The creative quality of your advertising depends on how well you work with your creative agencies. You need to guide them with your knowledge of the brand, the market and the consumer, while giving them the freedom to come up with groundbreaking ideas. Listening and collaboration skills are vital. Here are some tips for partnering creative agencies.

ENSURE EVERYONE IS ALIGNED WITH THE TASK

If you have developed a strong creative brief, your creative agency will know exactly how you want people to see your brand and the role that advertising needs to play. Before embarking on advertising development, you need to make sure your creative agency is fully on board with your thinking. It's worth asking them to give you their take. If they're fully aligned with your thinking, that's great. If they challenge you with a new thought that makes you stop and think, that's even better.

FOCUS ON THE 'BIG IDEA'

Given how fragmented the modern media environment is, brands need big ideas that work well across diverse channels and formats. A strong one-off TV ad is all very well but is of little use if it represents a dead end. 'Big ideas' lead to advertising that works well in print, outdoor, digital display and social media, as well as inspiring strong executions for years to come. For this reason, it's a good idea to ask your agency to articulate the underlying idea behind the advertising – the big idea that will connect ads across all media – and share examples of how the big idea could be brought to life in a variety of different channels. The greater the variety of storylines the agency comes up with that work well across different media channels, the better.

BE CLEAR ON THE BRAND'S ROLE

Creativity provides an opportunity for your advertising to drive sales, but only if it is harnessed for the brand's benefit. Lots of highly creative advertising captivates the audience but fails to involve the brand. When developing advertising with your agency, an important question to ask at every step of the process is:

'How will people remember our brand when they see/hear our advertising?' Brands can play a number of different roles in the advertising idea. What's important is that the advertising excels in at least one of these branding mechanisms. See Sections 7.4 and 8.5 for more ideas about how to assess whether your advertising will be well-branded or not.

2.4 COMBINING YOUR MEDIA

The evidence is clear that your advertising will be more effective if you use a combination of media. Binet and Field have shown that combining 'brand-building' and 'activation' media delivers the strongest ROI. Media experts will also tell you that in the best campaigns, the role of each channel is clearly defined and there is a plan for how they will work together – to maximize reach and create overlap if/when this is beneficial. For example, an ad campaign for the launch of a new car might include:

- Outdoor advertising with a humorous headline that neatly captures what's special about the car
- Print advertising that showcases the car's beauty and has a QR code that links to the website
- A website that makes the car seem even more exciting and makes it easy for visitors to book a test drive at their local dealership
- Advertising at the dealership showing how the car seamlessly incorporates state-of-the-art technology
- Emails to test drivers highlighting the great deals currently available

When marketers talk about integrated, 360-degree campaigns, this is what they mean. All encounters with the brand and its communications shape people's perceptions of the brand and influence whether they eventually buy it. Encounters related to competitor brands also have an influence. The 'Hankins Hexagon' was developed by extraordinary media thinker James Hankins in 2021. It highlights the many touchpoints people might encounter on their path to purchase and reminds us that different people are also likely to encounter different combinations of touchpoints.

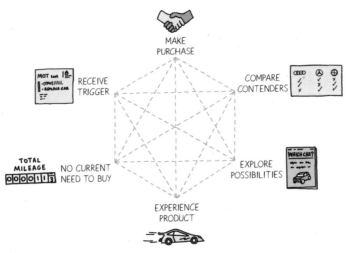

THE HANKINS HEXAGON
POTENTIAL STOP-OFFS ON THE PATH TO PURCHASE

Every category user starts with no current need to buy, because they have bought the category and what they bought still meets their needs. In fact, according to the Ehrenberg-Bass Institute, at any one time, 95% of category users are in this passive state. Their purchase journey only starts when they are triggered to buy again. This happens when you notice you are running dangerously low on cornflakes, your insurance is about to expire, or how much better your life would be if you had the latest smartphone. How people are influenced on their journey varies, depending on the paths they take and what they experience along the way. Some paths are more common than others, depending on the category. Here are some examples of the paths people might take in different circumstances.

HANKINS HEXAGON — PATH EXAMPLES

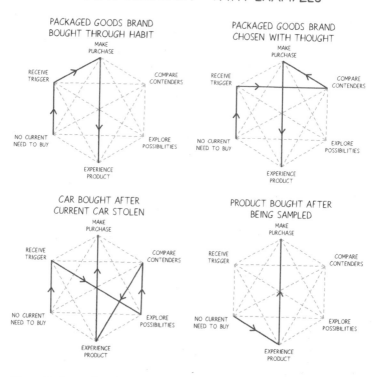

Given that people take different paths and encounter different content on their purchase journey, marketers need to make sure their brand is present, and comes across well, in all key touchpoints.

TIMING YOUR MEDIA

It is common practice to spend heavily on advertising during the early launch phase of a new product before settling down to a lower level afterwards. This helps to maximize sales early on so your distribution partners and retailers can see your product's potential. Assuming customers like the product and repeat purchasing levels are high, the early success of the product will give you and your operational partners the confidence to continue supporting it.

On the other hand, if your business plan is to start small and slowly crank up sales and production volumes, your advertising should follow a similar pattern.

Once your product/brand is well established, your next aim might be to achieve sustained, long-term growth. If so, invest in ongoing advertising, rather than concentrating all your spend in big, infrequent bursts. Spreading out your media spend means your brand will be a salient option whenever people enter the category or are about to buy it again. To illustrate this, consider two similar brands with the same annual advertising spend. BRAND A blows its budget in a single burst at the start of the year. BRAND B chooses to spread its spend across three bursts each year. This results in BRAND B being the more salient brand for most of the year.

CONCENTRATED VS SPREAD-OUT MEDIA EXAMPLE

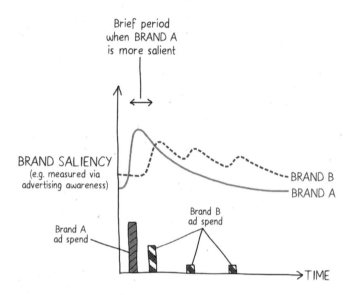

This illustration is based on multiple real-life examples from the UK confectionery market and is supported by an analysis of Kantar Millward Brown's global tracking database (Twose, 2019).

Spreading your spend continuously can be even more effective than bursts. Continuous spend minimizes the waste caused by diminishing returns (see Section 2.1).

CONTINUOUS AD SPEND IS MORE EFFICIENT THAN BURSTS

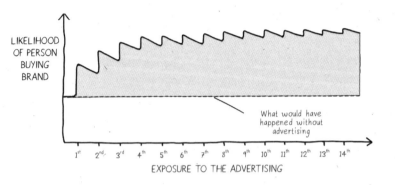

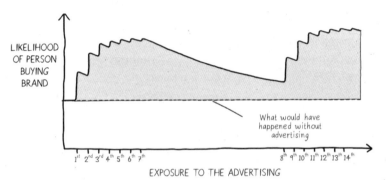

Concentrating your spend produces higher peaks in advertising impact but reduces the total effect. This is why savvy marketers tend to avoid media plans that would result in high exposure frequencies, capping frequencies around two times a week, technology permitting. Gijsenberg and Nijs (2019) confirmed that spreading out your media spend insulates your brand from competitors' actions and boosts sales.

When it comes to activation advertising designed to trigger people to choose your brand when they are buying the category, any seasonal peaks and troughs in category sales should be considered. For example, supermarket ice-cream sales occur all year round in the UK but are much higher during the summer and peak during Bank Holiday weekends. Ice-cream brands should match their activation spend to these patterns. Media costs also vary by season, and this can also influence when your brand should invest in order to maximise ROI.

Once a brand is well established, its sales may appear to be relatively stable, holding up well even during periods of lower advertising spend. If so, the marketing manager might be put under pressure to cut advertising spend for a prolonged period to reduce costs. This is certainly a good way of increasing profitability in the short term. Cutting ad spend allows you to cash in on the brand equity you have built up in previous years. The thinking is that if sales start to fall significantly, advertising spend can be restored to historic levels.

However, this is not what happens in practice. Sales models for brands that have 'gone dark' for a while indicate that the strategy makes bad economic sense in the long term.

COMMERCIAL IMPACT OF 'GOING DARK'

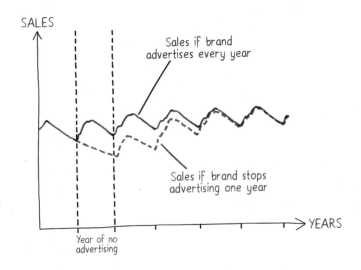

This case example was produced by modelling experts D2D (Draft-2Digital). It is based on a model for a brand that advertises every year. It shows the expected reduction in sales that would occur if the brand stopped spending for one year. In the long run, this drop was much bigger than the media money saved (although the brand would have made a slightly higher profit in the initial year). The model estimated that the brand would lose £1.7m from the bottom line in total, and it would take at least four years for sales to recover to historic levels.

2.6 TARGETING

In his seminal book *How Brands Grow*, Byron Sharp demonstrates beyond any doubt that penetration growth is key to long-term brand growth. The backbone of your media strategy should, therefore, be activity that reaches as many category users, and future users, as possible. This way, your campaign will grow penetration by encouraging existing customers to carry on using your brand and attracting new customers. Binet and Field analysed the database of award-winning, effective advertising held by the UK's Institute of Practitioners in Advertising. Their results show that campaigns targeting the whole market have a much bigger impact on the brand's market share than campaigns focused on existing customers or new customers.

BROAD REACH CAMPAIGNS GROW MARKET SHARE MORE

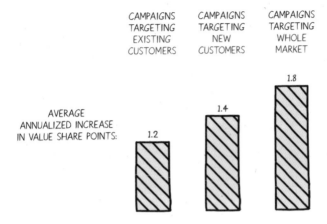

CAMPAIGNS TARGETING EXISTING CUSTOMERS

CAMPAIGNS TARGETING NEW CUSTOMERS

CAMPAIGNS TARGETING WHOLE MARKET

AVERAGE ANNUALIZED INCREASE IN VALUE SHARE POINTS:

1.2 1.4 1.8

If your brand caters for diverse groups of consumers with different needs, priorities and media habits, you might also want to invest in activity tailored to these groups. You will need to estimate whether the additional activity targeted at these segments will result in a sales gain that is enough to warrant the extra production and media costs.

MEDIA TARGETING PRINCIPLES

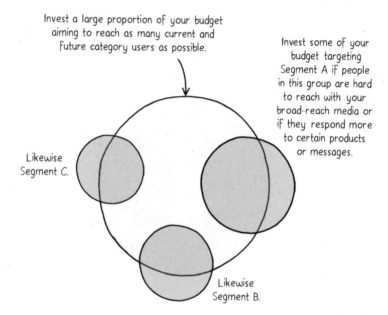

Invest a large proportion of your budget aiming to reach as many current and future category users as possible.

Invest some of your budget targeting Segment A if people in this group are hard to reach with your broad-reach media or if they respond more to certain products or messages.

Likewise Segment C.

Likewise Segment B.

Most media channels can be used to target specific segments, but their accuracy at doing so varies. With non-digital media such as linear TV and printed media, targeting is achieved by choosing the channels/publications and programs/sections that are known to reach people with a profile similar to your segment.

Some digital media (e.g., TikTok, Facebook) have in-depth information about their consumers, allowing you to target people with specific demographics, attitudes and behaviours. These are sometimes referred to as micro-targets. Micro-targeting allows you to serve tailored content to each segment. Whether this is worth doing depends on the time and cost of understanding what each segment will respond to best and developing tailored content for each segment. I suspect that AI-driven content will become increasingly compelling, making it quick and easy to produce tailored content and experiment with it cheaply. This would dramatically increase the viability, impact and cost-efficiency of an approach involving micro-targeting.

CHAPTER 3

PAID-FOR
ADVERTISING

INFLUENCER
PARTNERSHIPS

USING FOLLOWERS
TO SPREAD NEWS

GETTING FEEDBACK
FROM FOLLOWERS

PAID
MEDIA

3.1 CLASSIC MEDIA CHANNELS

CINEMA & TV

Cinema and TV provide an audio-visual experience at a time when the audience is generally attentive. People are waiting for their chosen content to start or restart and have few distractions. At the cinema, viewers have nothing to draw their attention away from the screen – apart from, perhaps, their popcorn or the person they came with. This means that advertising in these channels has a good opportunity to create strong memories connected with the brand that can influence purchase decisions in the long term. People watch ads in these channels for longer than most other channels (see Section 2.2) which makes it possible to tell stories – an effective way to create brand memories that last.

Unskippable YouTube has a lot in common with cinema and TV. Viewers are waiting for their video to start, and the level of external distraction is low. This explains why exposure durations are significantly longer than other social media channels.

To make the most of these channels, you will need to hire creative teams able to come up with and produce powerful content. Make sure your budget is enough to both create great content for these channels and to air it. If not, you'll need to use lower cost media options.

PRINT

Print is one of the oldest advertising media, dating back to the introduction of newspapers in the 1600s. Print media differs from cinema and TV in that the reader has control over how long they spend looking at an ad. As they flick through their publication, they will quickly skip over any ads that don't grab and hold their attention. This means that print ads need a visual hook to create enough immediate interest or intrigue to stop them turning the page. See Section 7 for more on this topic. An advantage of print media is that if you successfully draw people in, they can spend as long as they like reading about your product and why it's great.

OUTDOOR

Like most media, outdoor advertising can be used to fulfil many different roles. Whiskey brand Jack Daniels has used poster ads on the underground to tell memorable brand-building stories.

Outdoor advertising can also be used to activate brand memories just before people buy a category. For example, Wall's ice cream pays for outdoor ads like the one below to trigger positive brand memories as people walk into a shop that sells their ice creams.

OUTDOOR POINT OF SALE EXAMPLE

RADIO

Radio is often described as 'intimate.' DJs understand this and know how to make their audience feel warm and welcome, ready to hear about things that will resonate with them personally. Podcasts have the same effect. This creates an atmosphere that's hard to replicate in any other medium.

THE INTIMACY OF AUDIO

People usually listen to audio media when they are on their own. They are often doing something else at the same time – house-work, manual labour, jogging, driving or getting off to sleep. Since the level of distraction tends to be low, advertising in audio media can generate high levels of attention. When people are consuming audio content, they are actively looking for mental stimulation. It's an ideal opportunity for building brand memories.

Radio and podcast advertising is accessible to almost any brand because the entry-point costs are low. You could simply pay for the host of an audio program to mention or recommend your brand. Alternatively, you could invest in advertising. Production costs are low because they only involve recording voiceovers and using music/sound effects. Media costs can also be low if you partner with a single podcast or a local radio station. Many radio stations even offer free production for their advertisers. Your initial investment can focus on radio stations/podcasts that reach the most receptive segment of your target audience. You can extend the reach of your advertising by using more podcasts and radio stations as your budget increases.

3.2 SPONSORSHIP

Sponsorship means paying another organization to feature your brand name/logo in some of their marketing. Sponsorship enables a brand to sell to or communicate with the fans, followers, supporters or visitors of the entity being sponsored.

Sponsorships can range from:
- a local shop sponsoring the village fete
- a national brand sponsoring the country's favourite TV program
- a global brand sponsoring the Olympic Games

Reasons for using sponsorship fall into five main categories:

REASONS FOR SPONSORING

Increase brand
name/logo salience
 and

Reach a specific
target audience
 and

Enhance your
brand image
 and

Reinforce your
brand purpose
 and

Provide selling
opportunities
 and

INCREASE BRAND NAME/LOGO SALIENCE

Sponsorship can be a good way to increase or maintain the salience of your brand's name and logo. Car manufacturer Hyundai has sponsored a wide range of high-profile sports teams, events and organizations, including the FIFA World Cup, the Australian Open and the National Geographic Society, to increase brand name familiarity. Many new media channels have emerged over recent years resulting in few channels commanding a large audience on their own. Sponsorship of major sporting events remains an effective way to reach a mass audience, making it an attractive proposition for big brands. Global properties can be particularly appealing to international brands. Since these properties are understood in a similar way in every region, marketing campaigns to leverage the sponsorship can be developed centrally and used everywhere, with little need for local adaptation.

Sponsorship tends to work best for brands that are already well known and where the connection to the sponsored entity is obvious – BMW and motorsport teams in the Deutsche Tourenwagen Masters, for example.

The effect of sponsorship can be amplified by using it as an opportunity to tell stories about your brand or explain its features and benefits. These stories can be shared via social media and PR activities. For example, Nike often sponsors athletes during the Olympic Games. They create inspiring stories around these athletes, highlighting their journey, dedication and commitment to excellence. Nike shares these stories through short films or documentaries on social media platforms.

Sponsorships can also be used to extend the life of a marketing campaign by reminding people of the campaign via a key visual or slogan. From 2009 to 2012, Barclaycard sponsored the music festival Wireless, providing contactless payment wristbands to attendees. After the event, many people kept these branded wristbands as souvenirs, reminding them of the event and Barclaycard's sponsorship.

REACH A SPECIFIC TARGET AUDIENCE

Sponsorship can be an effective way to engage with target audiences that are otherwise hard to reach. Bulgari, a brand that makes luxury jewellery and watches, has often sponsored the Cannes Film Festival. The festival is attended by celebrities and high-net-worth individuals who are interested in film, fashion and luxury lifestyles. These people match Bulgari's target audience perfectly. Likewise, the well-known diapers brand Pampers has been a major sponsor of Mumsnet.com, a website dedicated to new parents. The sponsorship has included providing competition prizes, expert Q&A sessions, and contributing to the costs of live events.

ENHANCE YOUR BRAND IMAGE

If you have a clear idea about how you want people to think and feel about your brand, you can identify a sponsor to match these aspirations. Your brand will appropriate some of the sponsored brand's values by association. For example, by sponsoring Formula One, Rolex reinforces its status as a well-engineered, glamorous brand for the rich and famous. Sponsoring a popular or highly respected organization can enhance a brand's credibility. For example, the German supermarket chain Lidl has sponsored organizations in the UK such as the British Heart Foundation and The Prince's Trust. This has helped the brand become more widely accepted and respected among UK consumers.

REINFORCE YOUR BRAND PURPOSE

If your brand exists to fulfil a purpose, sponsoring relevant organizations is a good way to highlight your commitment to the cause. The outdoor equipment retailer Patagonia exists to help people enjoy the great outdoors while protecting it for future generations. The brand shows its commitment to this ideal by sponsoring a variety of individuals, athletes and organizations who share their passion for environmental and social activism, and who are involved in activities such as climbing, surfing, skiing and snowboarding.

PROVIDE SELLING OPPORTUNITIES

If you are a fast-food chain, a sponsorship deal with a sports organization might include exclusive rights to sell food at their events. The value of these sales should be factored into your decision about whether to become a sponsor. Sponsorship deals may also include the ability to leverage the customer database of the sponsored entity. This could be used, for example, to deliver advertising for your brand directly to fans of the brand you are sponsoring.

Sponsorships can also provide an opportunity to build relationships with people who are able to support your business goals. Inviting stakeholders to an exclusive event that your company sponsors can enhance your company's reputation and allow you to discuss concerns or potential partnerships.

While there are many good reasons for using sponsorship, there is a risk that the decision will be made for the wrong reasons. The CEO may be keen to sponsor an organization or event they are passionate about, but the deal won't always align with the best interests of the brand. Sponsorships have the potential to boost employee morale, but there may be better ways of using the money to achieve this. Marketers need to make sure that the sponsorships they invest in will fulfil a clearly identified strategic need.

3.3 PRODUCT PLACEMENT

Product placement involves paying for your brand to feature within a TV program, movie, video game or other content, to increase its awareness, appeal or credibility. As with sponsorship, global properties such as blockbuster Hollywood movies can work well for multinational brands. These movies are understood and appreciated the world over, which means that marketing and PR campaigns that exploit the product placement deal can be developed centrally and deployed easily within each region.

You might consider product placement if you have identified content that matches your target audience and desired brand associations. You could pay to advertise around this content, but product placement provides an opportunity to create a more memorable connection with the brand, depending on how and when it appears.

For maximum effectiveness, the brand should be featured in a prominent and memorable way when the audience is highly engaged in the content. Omega watches have featured in James Bond movies since *GoldenEye* in 1995. The watch is often showcased during the customary scene in which the famous secret agent is briefed by Q on the latest gadgets. Awareness of the

Omega brand and the appeal of their watches is strengthened by this association with the James Bond character and the role their watches play within the movies.

OMEGA PRODUCT PLACEMENT EXAMPLE

Scientific evidence about the effectiveness of product placements is scant. Practitioners believe that success depends on the following four factors. The brand needs to be prominent when it is featured and, ideally, be integral to the storyline or action. The content should be relevant to whatever the brand aims to be associated with, and the brand should be portrayed in such a way that people find it appealing.

PRODUCT PLACEMENT SUCCESS FACTORS

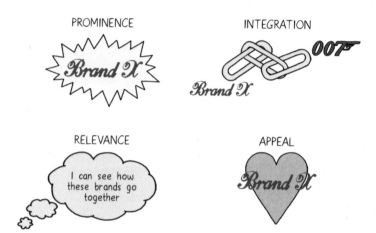

PROMINENCE

INTEGRATION

RELEVANCE

APPEAL

PROMINENCE

Brands encourage or pay for their products to be featured in movies and TV programmes. Apple is famous for giving computers, iPads and iPhones to production companies to use as props. This explains why iDevices appeared in 40% of movie box office hits in 2011, according to an analysis by Brandchannel. Apple even inverted its logo on its MacBooks so that it would appear upright to viewers when being used (despite this being counterintuitive for the users themselves – something Apple usually avoids).

However, having your product or logo visible doesn't guarantee people will notice it. Eye-tracking results show that people tend to look at whatever the director intended them to look at. Logos in the background are usually missed.

INTEGRATION

The brand is much more likely to be noticed and remembered if it plays an integral role in the storyline. Apple's PowerBook had a starring role in *Mission Impossible*, in return for the movie being featured in Apple's own advertising in the run up to its release. In 2021's *No Time to Die*, James Bond's Omega watch emits an electric pulse that disables a henchman's bionic eye – allowing Bond to save the day.

RELEVANCE

A brand should choose to place its products in content that will create the kinds of association the brand desires. In 1982, for example, Reese's Pieces were featured in the movie *E.T.* They were the candy that the adorable extra-terrestrial loved to eat. The placement reinforces the idea that Reese's Pieces are a comforting sweet treat for children. This resulted in a significant increase in sales for the brand.

Less relevant sponsorships have little chance of being effective. Mercedes Benz surprised everyone in 2015 by partnering with Nintendo to have its cars feature in the popular video games *Mario Kart* and *Super Mario Maker*.

MERCEDES PRODUCT PLACEMENT EXAMPLE

According to a spokesperson for the car manufacturer, the product placement was designed to strengthen brand awareness and appeal among people in their 30s and 40s, many of whom play Mario games regularly and hold strong affection for the Mario universe. The partnership was short-lived. *Mario Kart* may be fast-paced and exciting, but Mario isn't exactly stylish and sophisticated, making the partnership ill-judged.

APPEAL

Ultimately, the way the brand is portrayed in the placement should make it appealing to the audience. In the famous 80s movie *Back to the Future*, futuristic Pepsi products and branding is displayed throughout the movie, making the brand seem popular, cool and enduring.

Product placement can be very expensive. If executed well, it should have a bigger impact on your brand than advertising – but only amont fans of the content. Given that reach strategies tend to outperform depth strategies (see Section 2.6) you need to consider whether the money you'd spend on product placement might be better spent on other media able to achieve broader reach.

3.4 SOCIAL MEDIA

Major social media platforms offer advertisers the opportunity to reach many consumers. Facebook, for example, claimed to have 3 billion active monthly users in January 2023 – more than one third of the world's population.

Social media platforms can be used in several ways.

WAYS OF USING SOCIAL MEDIA

PAID-FOR
ADVERTISING

INFLUENCER
PARTNERSHIPS

USING FOLLOWERS
TO SPREAD NEWS

GETTING FEEDBACK
FROM FOLLOWERS

PAID-FOR ADVERTISING

This works like other paid-for media channels. You select your audience profile and pay for your posts to be exposed as people browse their content feeds, regardless of whether they follow you. These are known as sponsored posts. You need to bear in mind that exposure durations are typically short – about one or two seconds. People tend to scroll quickly past most of the ads, looking for posts from their friends and family. Using videos that were created with TV in mind are rarely effective. See Chapters 7 and 8 for thoughts on how to create ads that work in just a few seconds.

Paid-for social media advertising works best when your objective is to keep your brand at the top of people's minds so that they are more likely to choose it when they next buy the category. Famous brands with well-established distinctive assets (see Chapter 6) have an advantage since they can jog people's memories within seconds by featuring their assets early on during the ad. Other brands need to find a way to hook people in within the first few seconds, so they watch the ads for long enough to convey the brand and something memorable about it. See Section 8.1 for more on this.

New ways of using social media to sell products are continually emerging. 'Social Commerce' combines social media and e-commerce. If an Instagram user likes the look of a pair of sunglasses worn by a model in a post, they can click on it, learn more about the item and buy it without leaving the platform. Social media marketplaces allow users to buy and sell products using a platform managed by the social media provider. Social media storefronts enable businesses to set up their own online stores through which to sell directly to consumers.

INFLUENCER PARTNERSHIPS

If there are influencers that have built a large following on social media by talking about a topic that relates to your brand, there may be an opportunity to partner with them. Collaborations with influencers help to build credibility and interest among 'early adopters,' who can help to spread positive word of mouth to other consumers. See Section 3.5 for more details.

USING FOLLOWERS TO SPREAD NEWS

You can use your social media channels to share news related to your brand. For example, you can publish stories designed to enhance your brand's reputation or to announce a product launch or promotion. In most cases, the coverage will be small compared to other PR and paid-for advertising vehicles. If, however, your brand has a large following and people are interested in the category, the free coverage can be significant (e.g., Apple or Tesla/Elon Musk).

GETTING FEEDBACK FROM FOLLOWERS

Your social media followers tend to be fans of your brand. Listening to their comments and asking them questions about existing or future products is a good source of information and inspiration. Remember, however, that the attitudes and preferences of your followers will not necessarily represent those of your wider target audience.

3.5 INFLUENCERS

From a marketing point of view, an influencer is someone with a large following who engages regularly with their audience, particularly via social media. Many influencers are prepared to publicize a brand in return for a fee. Brands usually partner influencers who are known for their knowledge or passion for relevant topics. For example, Joy Wilson, known as Joy the Baker, is a food blogger and cookbook author who has partnered with KitchenAid. She has created recipes using KitchenAid products and appeared in the company's promotional videos. Sephora collaborates with beauty influencers to promote their latest makeup and skincare products to beauty enthusiasts and makeup lovers. Choosing influencers who are an authority in an area related to what the brand stands for makes the endorsement credible and ensures the audience will fit well with the brand's needs.

The term Brand Ambassador is often used for an influencer who is famous for something that isn't directly related to the brand but is relevant to the desired identity. BMW, for example, has partnered with Alexandra Lapp, the entrepreneur and blogger, famous for her love of fashion and travel.

The most popular influencers have hundreds of thousands of followers making them among the biggest media channels in the world.

REASONS FOR PARTNERING AN INFLUENCER

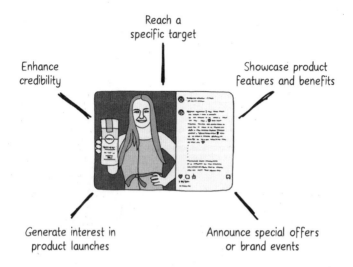

Reach a
specific target

Enhance
credibility

Showcase product
features and benefits

Generate interest in
product launches

Announce special offers
or brand events

Partnering influencers works well for building awareness of new products and special offers because influencers are always on the lookout for news to share with their followers. It also works well for products that require an explanation in order for consumers to understand their value. Influencers can explain how a product works and provide demonstrations that might be less interesting and convincing if included in traditional ads.

The soft drinks brand Prime was launched in January 2022. It is promoted by influencers Logan Paul and KSI. According to an article in TheConversation.com (2023), the brand achieved sales worth 250 million US dollars in its first year. In the UK, supermarkets had to restrict sales of the brand due to stock shortages and, at one point, 12-packs of the drink sold via online resellers for more than £1,000.

PRIME HYDRATION INFLUENCER EXAMPLE

LOGAN PAUL
(23m YouTube subscribers)

KSI
(24m YouTube subscribers)

PRIME
($250m sales in first year)

The phenomenal success of the brand's launch can be attributed to the popularity of the influencers – between them, they have over 40 million YouTube subscribers. Their ability to engage their audience and amplify the reach of their videos (e.g., by inviting other famous YouTubers to try Prime) enabled Prime to establish global fame and spectacular sales within just a few months – something that few brands have ever achieved. The hype surrounding Prime will almost certainly have died down by the time this book reaches the shelves. Fashionable brands can quickly become passé. However, there have been cases of celebrity-driven brands that have gone on to achieve major, long-term success, such as Chuck Taylor's Converse All-Star sports shoes and Beats headphones by Dr. Dre.

3.6 DIRECT ADVERTISING

Direct advertising is where brands communicate directly with their target audience through channels such as postal services, emails, texts or phone calls. To leverage direct advertising, brands need access to contact details for relevant consumers. They need residential addresses ('direct mail'), emails or phone numbers. These could come from the company's own database, built when customers registered their purchases or when people have signed up to notifications via the brand's website, app or one of its promotions. Lists of relevant individuals can also be bought from companies that compile contact information for people or businesses that fit specific criteria. These lists can be based on demographics (such as age, gender, income level, job-types), geographic location, hobbies/interests or purchasing habits.

Direct advertising is designed to encourage a specific action from its recipients. Actions include visiting a website, calling to make an enquiry or attending a live event. Content can take different forms such as letters, emails, text messages, newsletters, flyers, catalogues or brochures.

DIRECT MAIL EXAMPLE

According to the Data and Marketing Association (see Ivana V., 2023), the average response rate for postal direct mail in 2021 was 5% for lists based on the brand's broad target audience. Mailchimp (2019), a world leading email marketing company, claims to achieve a response rate of 3%. These figures compare favourably with data from Smartinsights.com (2023), which quotes click-through rates for Facebook (1.1%), Instagram (0.2%) and Google digital display (0.05%), and are similar to those of paid search advertising (6%).

Response rates vary depending on how the direct advertising is executed. People put the envelope in the recycling bin or delete the email unless the content quickly piques their interest. The example in the image above isn't groundbreaking, but it does give people a reason to open the envelope. It is well worth investing time and effort to ensure your direct advertising grabs people's attention. You could easily achieve double the response rate and generate impressive sales results.

Direct advertising works best as an activation medium (see Section 2.4). People are more responsive to direct advertising if they are already familiar with and interested in the brand, thanks to brand-building media. Direct advertising, therefore, works best if it is used as part of a 360-degree campaign.

3.7 SEARCH

When people are thinking about buying something, they often search for information or opinions to guide their choice. This is more common for categories with high ticket prices or ones that consumers find interesting. If someone already has a brand in mind, they may search for it directly. According to research I conducted in 2015, in conjunction with Omaid Hiwaizi from visual search experts Blippar, about one in ten of all searches are related to shopping. This amounts to billions of searches every year. Marketers need to determine how to leverage search for the benefit of their brand.

When people make shopping-related searches, they use various platforms including search engines, online marketplaces, department stores and supermarkets. Major search platforms in 2023 include Google, Bing, Yahoo, Baidu, Amazon, eBay, Taobao and Tmall (popular in China), Rakuten (popular in Japan), Flipkart (popular in India), and Mercados Libre (popular in Latin America).

PAID SEARCH

Marketers can pay to have their brand appear at the top of the search engine results pages (SERPs) when people search for chosen terms, or 'keywords.' This is known as search advertising, paid search or sponsored search. It is an example of intent-based targeting. It works well for categories where people research and/or make their purchase online. Advertisers usually choose keywords that indicate that the person searching is interested in buying the category.

SEARCH KEYWORD EXAMPLES

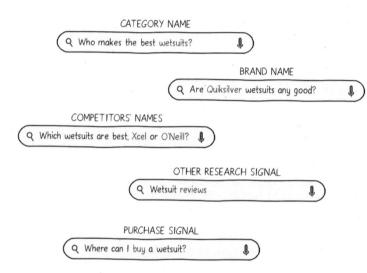

CATEGORY NAME

Q Who makes the best wetsuits?

BRAND NAME

Q Are Quiksilver wetsuits any good?

COMPETITORS' NAMES

Q Which wetsuits are best, Xcel or O'Neill?

OTHER RESEARCH SIGNAL

Q Wetsuit reviews

PURCHASE SIGNAL

Q Where can I buy a wetsuit?

Paying for your ads to appear at the top of search results when people search for your brand name may be worthwhile if you are a small business. After all, your competitors may have paid so that their ads appear whenever people search for your brand. However, well-known brands won't need to pay for advertising to appear when people put their name into a search because they are likely to organically feature high up in search results. In March 2012, eBay conducted an experiment to test the theory. According to the *Harvard Business Review* (2013), the company stopped paying for search ads containing the word 'eBay' on Yahoo and Bing search engines but continued to on Google. They found that sales coming via Yahoo and Bing were unaffected. Instead of clicking on paid links, consumers used the organic search listing slightly lower down the page.

At the time of writing, the world's leading search engine, Google, offers 22 different ways to promote your brand.

The cost of search advertising depends on:
- how many other companies are bidding on the same keywords
- how effective your ad will be at getting people to click on it (estimated by Google's AI)
- how engaging and user-friendly your website is (based on usage statistics)

Google wants to ensure its users find what they're looking for, so it charges less for advertising that consumers find relevant and leads to positive experiences. This means that having a well-targeted search ad and a compelling website reduces your media costs.

According to Google's AI, the most effective ads have these characteristics:
- Feature the brand/product name to trigger the brand's mental associations
- Include the keyword in the text, so that people can quickly see that the ad is relevant
- Summarize what the product is/does and what sets it apart, ideally via a catchy phrase
- Provide a compelling reason to click ('call to action')
- Only attract clicks from people for whom the brand is relevant

The UK insurance price comparison site CompareTheMarket.com came up with an ingenious way to leverage search while minimizing spend. They created a fictional website, CompareTheMeerkat.com, and created a tongue-in-cheek campaign to promote it. This resulted in people making searches containing the word 'meerkat,' a search term that is 100 times cheaper than the word 'market.' Of course, the CompareTheMeerkat.com website quickly re-directed people to CompareTheMarket.com, but the trick allowed the company to make enormous savings.

SEARCH ENGINE OPTIMIZATION

Search engine optimization, or SEO, involves making changes to your website so that it appears higher up on the results page(s) when people search for something related to your brand. These changes also reduce the cost of search advertising because search engines want their users to be directed to relevant sites with a good user experience.

SEO changes might include:

- Using keywords throughout your site (i.e., the terms people use most often when making searches related to your category.)
- Ensuring your site is appealing, clear and easy for visitors to navigate. The goal is to reduce your site's 'bounce rate' – the proportion of people who enter the site and then exit it without any interaction.
- Having a logical structure that makes it easy for search engine 'bots' to analyse and categorize the content. Giving each page a name that describes its contents and including title tags, meta descriptions, headings and internal links can all help.
- Asking partner organizations to include links to your site. This increases your site's credibility in the eyes of the search engine's algorithm, especially if your partners' sites have a large audience.

Paid search advertising is a great way to activate brand memories and remind people about your brand at a time when they are thinking about buying the category. It is particularly valuable for brands that are widely bought online because the ads can provide a link that allows people to buy the brand within a few clicks. However, search ads are not well-suited to brand building since they are mainly text-based and offer little opportunity to build strong memories around the brand.

CHAPTER 4

L.　E.　G.　S.

LAUGH OUT LOUD　EDGY　GRIPPING　SEXY

EARNED AND OWNED MEDIA

4.1 REVIEWS AND RATINGS

There is strong evidence that reviews and ratings for products and services have a big influence on brand choice, especially in categories where people research different options before buying.

- Products with 50+ reviews have a conversion rate 5% higher than products with fewer than five (Spiegel Research Center, 2017)
- Most consumers will only use a local business if it has a star rating of four or more (Marchant, 2014)
- Restaurants have revenues that are 5-9% higher for every one-star increase in their Yelp ratings (Harvard Business School, 2016)

This should be no surprise to marketers. Great products and excellent customer service are major drivers of sustainable profit growth and lead to positive reviews and ratings. If your brand delivers a superior experience, remind customers to leave reviews and make it quick and easy for them to do so. You can do this by handing out 'thank-you-for-your-business' cards or sending follow-up emails or texts. If the praise comes flooding in, amplify its effect by highlighting it in your paid or owned media. Social Proof of this kind can be highly persuasive.

WHICH WOULD YOU CHOOSE?

Rad-Dab X100 DAB+ Radio, Recharchable Battery and Mains Powered with USB charging

⭐⭐⭐⭐⭐ 2,523

£42⁹⁹

Dab-Rad 2500 DAB+ Radio, Recharchable Battery and Mains Powered with USB charging

⭐⭐⭐⭐⭐ 2,764

£38⁹⁹

It pays to monitor reviews for your brand and respond quickly and professionally to any criticism, aiming to put matters right whenever appropriate. If you receive consistently poor reviews, make it a priority to understand the problems and fix them. As previously shown, even the best advertising cannot compensate for a bad product.

4.2 MOBILIZING YOUR FANS

All brands should aim to leverage positive endorsements from customers to give other people confidence in the brand, but some brands put advocacy at the heart of their marketing strategy.

Novel or disruptive brands often use customer referral schemes to help overcome consumer uncertainty or scepticism. These schemes offer customers cash, discounts or free products for recruiting new users. Examples include ride sharing company Uber, food delivery service Grubhub, accommodation sharing brand Airbnb, electric car manufacturer Tesla and meal kit delivery services HelloFresh and Blue Apron.

Other brands aim to deliver an exceptional user experience that customers will spontaneously tell their friends about. Athletic clothing company Lululemon offers free yoga classes in their stores. Cosmetics brand Lush has basins in its stores to show their fizzy bath bombs in action. Online apparel retailer Zappos delivers a customer service experience that goes above and beyond to generate word of mouth. In one case, a call went on for over ten hours because the customer needed someone to talk to. In the end, they bought a pair of Ugg boots, and the record-breaking call made the news.

If your brand is aligned with a societal cause that your customers care about, this can provide inspiration for marketing content your fans are likely to share. Ben & Jerry's, Patagonia and Dove are famous examples. The success of direct-to-consumer cosmetics company Glossier highlights how a marketing strategy leveraging the power of earned media can be effective.

GLOSSIER BRAND ADVOCACY EXAMPLE

GLOSSIER REPS

INSTAGRAMMABILITY

COMMUNITY VALUES

GLOSSIER REPS
Customers can receive free products if they publicize the brand to their network of friends and followers.

INSTAGRAMMABILITY
Glossier develops products, packaging and social media posts that their fans want to share with their followers. This helps Glossier reach a large audience via word of mouth (earned media).

COMMUNITY VALUES
Glossier celebrates inclusivity, individuality and natural beauty – values that resonate with many of its customers. This helps mobilize existing fans to advocate for the brand and to attract new, like-minded customers.

4.3 AIMING FOR VIRAL EXPOSURE

While mobilizing fans can bring huge benefits to a brand, companies aiming to promote their brand by generating viral exposure to their content are gambling on a risky strategy. Some brands do have a lucky streak with content that was designed to go viral and succeeds in doing so. Their chances of sustained growth, however, are small. No professional brand manager should build a marketing strategy based on this approach.

The facts are clear. Very few marketing initiatives go viral. An analysis by market research company Kantar Millward Brown (2011) found that 96% of US ads achieve a trivial number of organic views on YouTube.

VERY FEW ADS GO VIRAL

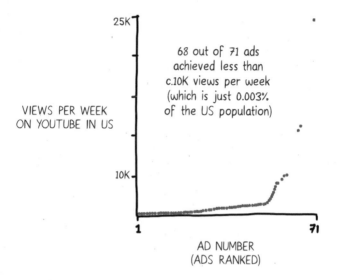

25K

68 out of 71 ads
achieved less than
c.10K views per week
(which is just 0.003%
of the US population)

VIEWS PER WEEK
ON YOUTUBE IN US

10K

1   71

AD NUMBER
(ADS RANKED)

Only about 1 in 100 ads achieve significant coverage from 'free' views, and these ads tend to have already benefited from 'seeding.' Seeding is the investment made by an advertiser to kick-start exposures to an ad so that it appears in 'Trending Videos' lists, encouraging further views.

The experiences of UK chocolate manufacturer Cadbury from 2007 to 2009 illustrate why brands cannot rely on viral exposure for long-term success. In 2007, Cadbury aired its famous 'Gorilla' ad. It featured a gorilla playing the opening drum sequence from Phil Collins' hit 'In the Air Tonight.' The ad was bizarre, mesmerizing and highly shareable. It was also profitable – if you factor in distribution gains and price effects. Cadbury tried several times to replicate this success but without much luck (e.g., 'Airport Trucks' in 2008 and 'Eyebrow Dance' in 2009).

If you feel that your only option is to gamble on creating content that might go viral, it's worth knowing the characteristics known to make it more likely. An analysis I conducted during my time at research company Kantar Millward Brown (2011) identified the characteristics of video ads that achieved high levels of exposure due to social sharing. These videos tended to score exceptionally highly in at least one of these four areas, often in several of them. These are what give videos the 'legs' to go viral.

CHARACTERISTICS OF CONTENT THAT GOES VIRAL

L.   E.   G.   S.

LAUGH OUT LOUD   EDGY   GRIPPING   SEXY

4.4 AMPLIFYING USER-GENERATED CONTENT

User-generated content means anything featuring a brand that has been created by the public. It is usually an image or video, shared on social media. This could be an homage to the brand, a parody of its advertising or simply an incidental reference. Most of this content is seen by just a handful of people. From time to time, however, it goes viral and becomes a meme – in other words, it becomes known by the population at large. If you are luckily enough for your brand to be featured in user-generated content that captures the public's imagination, be ready to amplify its coverage.

A film showing the explosive results of mixing Mentos mints with Diet Coke was uploaded in 2005. Entertainment company Eepybird.com filmed their own version of the experiment, and their video triggered thousands of people to film and share the results of similar experiments. The Mentos marketing team acted quickly to keep it going. They provided Eepybird with free Mentos and cash to fund further experiments and produce more films. The confectionery manufacturer claimed that the free publicity generated by these videos was worth in the region of $10m, roughly half of what the brand would normally spend on advertising in the US each year.

COKE AND MENTOS MEME 2005

Ocean Spray pulled off a similar trick more recently. In September 2020, a factory worker from Idaho named Nathan Apodaca skateboarded to work when his truck wouldn't start. On the way, he filmed himself swigging from a bottle of Ocean Spray while miming along to 'Dream' by Fleetwood Mac. He later posted the film on TikTok. The video has received over 30 million views by the time of writing and inspired hundreds of copies. Ocean Spray amplified the brand benefit by generating additional publicity, e.g., by giving Nathan a new truck full of cranberry juice cartons. It's hard to engineer this kind of publicity, but if it happens spontaneously, your Marketing and PR teams need to respond quickly and boldly to make the most of the opportunity.

Beyond viral advertising, many brands use their websites and social media accounts to encourage consumers to create and share content. Sports camera maker GoPro picks up on posts containing #GoPro that show off the kinds of amazing sporting feats their cameras can capture. Airbnb has a dedicated Instagram account (@airbnbexperiences) for its customers to share moments from their unique travel experiences. These kinds of activity can help your brand attract an army of fans. The number of fans may be trivial compared to the brand's entire target audience, but their combined network can be significant.

4.5 LEVERAGING OWNED MEDIA

Owned media are any touchpoints controlled by your company that customers and potential customers are exposed to. They include:

- Physical stores
- Display units within other retailers' stores
- Online stores
- Websites/blogs/social media accounts
- Brand apps
- Vehicles used for transportation

Owned media can be leveraged in multiple ways. Here are three of the most common:

WAYS TO LEVERAGE YOUR OWNED MEDIA

BOOST MENTAL AVAILABILITY

ALLOW POTENTIAL CUSTOMERS TO LEARN MORE

IMPOROVE ACCESS TO YOUR PRODUCT

BOOST MENTAL AVAILABILITY

If you have a network of physical stores, your storefronts and interior spaces provide a good opportunity to showcase your products to people passing by or entering your stores. The vehicles you use to distribute your products also provide an opportunity to boost your brand's mental availability. The sides of your vans and lorries should always feature your brand's logo prominently, possibly alongside a core brand message. Brands should treat every touchpoint as a promotion opportunity. Owned media can deliver significant coverage at minimal cost.

ALLOW POTENTIAL CUSTOMERS TO LEARN MORE

Every brand should have a website, mobile app or both, to give people who have heard about your brand an opportunity to discover more about it. The best websites and apps provide a slick, compelling experience that allows consumers to easily obtain the information they are looking for, while highlighting what makes the brand special. The best sites entice visitors by providing free, fun distractions. The most effective distractions are entertaining but also highlight the benefits of the brand's products or services. Most websites and apps, however, receive only a trickle of visitors. They come into their own when paid-for advertising is used to capture the attention of prospective customers, encouraging them to visit the website or download the app to learn more about the brand.

IMPROVE ACCESS TO YOUR PRODUCT

If you have your own physical or online stores, these help to boost your brand's physical availability beyond other distribution channels you have secured. Brands such as Wall's ice cream, Dunkin' Donuts and Coca-Cola invest heavily in fridges and freezers to ensure their products are physically available, and in tip-top condition, when consumers want to buy the category. Mobile apps can also make it easier to access brands. Anyone with the brand's app on their phone can buy its products or services in just a few clicks.

Most brands find that leveraging their owned media is a good investment. After all, the costs are low. You just need to produce the creative; there is no cost for achieving exposure. However, owned media like apps and websites tend to reach existing customers rather than future prospects. Brands seeking long-term growth need to attract a wide cross-section of buyers, so relying heavily on owned media is often a mistake.

4.6 PRODUCT AND PACKAGING

In many categories, the brand people have chosen is visible to other potential customers. Laptops, cars, clothing and accessories are prominent examples. Brands including Gucci, Apple and BMW all make sure their logo is prominent on their products. This ensures that every time people see their products, it provides an opportunity to raise brand saliency and interest. If you see a cool person sporting a Gucci logo, you can't help but be reminded of the brand and how cool it is.

If your brand has an appealing aesthetic design, you may be able to exploit this to enhance your brand's prominence at point of sale. Stock cube brand Oxo helped their brand stand out on the shelf by putting the letters O and X on one side of their packs to create an impactful shelf display that spelled 'OXO'. Dyson's in-store displays are equally impressive. They showcase the beautiful designs of their products by displaying them as if they were works of art in a gallery, setting them apart from other brands and helping to justify their premium prices. Nespresso also does a great job with their store-within-a-store displays, creating multicolour wall displays with their capsules that grab the eye, are appealing, and make the brand feel cool and sophisticated.

Exclusive US department store Bloomingdale's has enhanced its notoriety by encouraging customers to consider Bloomingdale's bags as status symbols. Being seen with one of their bags gives the customer social status and promotes the brand to their peers.

BLOOMINGDALE'S LITTLE BROWN BAG

Sports shoe brand Nike benefits hugely from having its 'Swoosh' logo prominent on all its shoes. I spent several days on the streets of London and its underground system trying to estimate how many times an average commuter would see the Nike logo in a year. It's probably over 200,000. These exposures have a very small impact on brand choice, but they add up. We are a social species. If lots of other people choose a particular brand, we tend to think it must be a good choice due to a powerful psychological phenomenon known as Social Proof (see Section 1.3).

THE BENEFIT OF BRANDING YOUR PRODUCTS

CHAPTER 5

CREATIVE APPROACH

5.1 CREATIVE FRAMEWORKS

Developing advertising creative can be messy, frustrating and confusing. Different teams have their own approaches, and the terminology is varied and ill-defined. People often talk at cross purposes. Here is one way of thinking about what's involved in creative development, expressed using my preferred terminology.

INSIGHT
An insight, or 'human truth,' is an observation about life that resonates with consumers. Some brands have identified an insight that they use to inspire the development of all brand-created encounters.

BRAND IDEA
This stems from the insight but is a specific way of expressing it, involving the brand and reflected in all brand communications. It is also referred to as the brand's 'Big Idea.'

CREATIVE IDEA
This is one of the ideas the creatives have come up with for bringing the brand idea to life in a compelling way. The phrases 'creative platform' and 'campaign idea' are sometimes used to mean something similar, although a creative idea can be the same across multiple campaigns.

EXECUTIONS

These are ways of executing the creative idea, destined to become ads in a specific channel and country.

TAGLINE

A phrase that encapsulates the brand idea. Also known as a brand line, strapline, slogan, catchphrase or motto. For more on taglines, see Section 6.5.

Advertising for the chocolate bar Snickers can be analysed using this framework.

SNICKERS CREATIVE FRAMEWORK

BRAND IDEA: Eating a Snickers when we're hungry restores us to our best, normal selves

CREATIVE IDEA: People tranformed into someone else due to hunger, recovered by Snickers

EXECUTION:

TAGLINE:

YOU'RE
NOT YOU
WHEN YOU'RE
HUNGRY

SNICKERS

Brands rarely develop advertising by working step by step through a process like this. Toiletries brand Dove, for example, discovered a powerful insight and brand idea after several decades of advertising. Some brands, like Coca-Cola, produce highly creative and effective advertising without basing it on a clear insight and brand idea. The framework is useful, however, for helping brand teams consider how they might take their advertising to the next level. There are two benefits of developing a creative framework for your brand.

INSPIRATION

Having a strong brand idea, based on an insight consumers identify with, can make it easier for you and your creative and media partners to come up with great ideas for how to advertise your brand across a whole range of channels. Snickers has produced thousands of wonderful videos, print, outdoor, radio and social media ads, all based on the same powerful brand idea.

CONSISTENCY

Consistency in the ideas, message and creative elements a brand uses helps to make the brand clear and strong in consumers' minds. The benefit of developing all your brand's advertising using the same creative framework is that all your content is sure to be consistent.

Advertising consistency is vital for long-term brand success. There are at least four ways to ensure that all your advertising content builds a consistent brand identity.

DIFFERENT WAYS TO ENSURE CONSISTENCY

WAY OF THINKING
The brand conveys its mission, values or guiding philosophy in all of its advertising.

'Just Do It'

'Campaign for Real Beauty'

PRODUCT PROMISE
All ads reinforce the benefit that the brand delivers.

'The Ultimate Driving Machine'

'Big on Quality, LIDL on Price'

STORY FORMAT
All ads use a similar story format to convey their message.

'The Axe Effect'

'Should've gone to 'Specsavers''

DISTINCTIVE STYLE
All ads have a distinctive look and feel that belong to the same 'brand world'.

'Undeniably Peculiar'

'Red Bull gives you wiings'

WAY OF THINKING

Brands using this approach are often described as 'purpose driven.' They have chosen to champion a way of thinking or publicize a cause and to reflect this in their advertising. This strategy works best if the ideas your brand stands for are connected to what the brand's products do. Nike manufactures sportswear, so it makes sense for them to inspire people to push through their barriers and take action to achieve their goals. Dove makes beauty products, so people can see the relevance of their stance to help all women feel good about the way they look. The brand needs to be committed to the cause and in it for the long run, ensuring its business practices are always consistent with the values it communicates. Any hypocrisy will be exposed quickly and communicated widely via social media.

PRODUCT PROMISE

A good way to link all your communications together and make it easy for them to reinforce the brand in people's minds is to base them on brand promise. BMW has been promising to provide 'The Ultimate Driving Machine' since 1974. Almost all BMW ads since then have brought this idea to life or supported it through product features. LIDL promises that its customers can always expect high quality at a low price – something the brand delivers thanks to its cost-efficient business model.

STORY FORMAT

This refers to brands that tell the same basic story about themselves in all their ads but execute it in a variety of ways. The male grooming brand Axe, known in some countries as Lynx, enjoyed huge success from the late 90s onward by telling the story of how a nerdy young man would become irresistible to women after using the brand. The transformation was attributed to 'The Axe Effect.' UK opticians Specsavers have produced hundreds of clever, amusing and memorable ads in which someone has made a major mistake because of their poor eyesight. They should, of course, have gone to Specsavers. Story formats make ads easier for people to understand and remember. They also make it easy for people to link the ad with the brand – provided the brand plays a clear role in the story.

DISTINCTIVE STYLE

Using a distinctive style is arguably the riskiest way to glue your advertising together and make it stick to your brand. It can work well, but the style must be highly distinctive. Hendrick's gin has created a look and feel that is truly unique and this has become closely linked with the brand. Their ads feature Victorian-style curiosities and contraptions, language and fonts, and lots of cucumbers and roses – the flavours that made the brand famous. Red Bull has used the same hand-drawn cartoon style since 1992. The distinctive look of these animations has helped the brand stand out in a highly competitive category. For more about using a distinctive creative style as a distinctive brand asset, see Section 6.3.

It is worth noting that most campaigns that employ these consistency-boosting strategies use a tagline that encapsulates the idea connecting all the ads. See section 6.5 for more about the benefits of taglines. Brands can also combine these strategies to amplify the unifying effect. Red Bull, for example, leverages at least three out of four.

5.2 HOW TO COME UP WITH A CREATIVE FRAMEWORK

A powerful creative framework is a rarity. If you find one, it should be cherished. The trick is to look for an insight that is within the small intersection between your brand's strengths and your potential customers' concerns.

FINDING AN INSIGHT YOUR BRAND COULD LEVERAGE

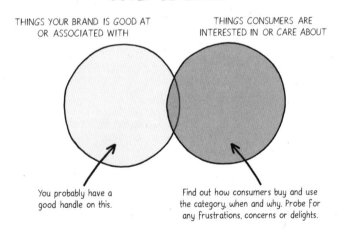

THINGS YOUR BRAND IS GOOD AT OR ASSOCIATED WITH

THINGS CONSUMERS ARE INTERESTED IN OR CARE ABOUT

You probably have a good handle on this.

Find out how consumers buy and use the category, when and why. Probe for any frustrations, concerns or delights.

Assuming you understand your brand well, there are several ways you might discover this illusive insight.

ETHNOGRAPHY

Ethnography involves observing people as they go about their daily life, probing to understand more about their habits and attitudes related to the category. Research of this kind can be time consuming and expensive but there is no better way to understand what consumers care about. Powerful insights often emerge from ethnographic research.

QUALITATIVE RESEARCH

Qualitative interviews often start with a general discussion about the category before focusing on a specific area. These preambles can reveal behaviours or attitudes that resonate with many category users. If you have the budget for it, there is a more creative alternative to traditional qualitative research you might consider. Improvisational theatre troupes such as The Second City offer a way to bring consumers' lives, needs and priorities to life through drama and comedy. Real consumers are interviewed by the actors to understand what's important to them and what role the category plays in their lives. The actors then devise and perform sketches that highlight these priorities and reveal the human truths behind them.

BREAK-THROUGH ADS

Occasionally, a brand will produce an ad or a series of ads that performs much better than normal. This could be because the advertising used an insight that captures the audience's imagination. If so, there may be an opportunity to leverage the insight in future ads and campaigns.

5.3 ADVERTISING INTERNATIONAL BRANDS

Taking your brand to overseas markets can bring many advantages. Producing and delivering products and services internationally can be more efficient due to economies of scale. Product components can be purchased at lower prices and operational systems bought and run centrally can be used internationally without significant additional cost. The same can apply to marketing: great advertising developed in one market often works equally well in other countries. However, there are no guarantees. An analysis of pre-test results by research company Kantar Millward Brown shows that even exceptional ads won't necessarily do well when exported to other countries (Twose, 2019, p199).

ADVERTISING DOESN'T ALWAYS TRAVEL WELL

How do exceptional ads perform
when tested in another country?

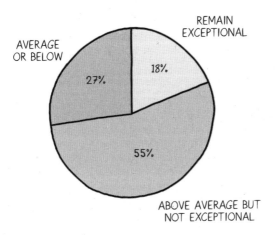

REMAIN EXCEPTIONAL
18%

AVERAGE OR BELOW
27%

ABOVE AVERAGE BUT NOT EXCEPTIONAL
55%

While cultures vary, there are some experiences and themes that are shared the world over. Brands that draw on these concepts in their advertising and bring them to life in a way that people from all countries can recognize are able to produce advertising that works well in all markets with little or no adaptation. Here are some themes that are known to transcend cultural boundaries.

THEMES THAT WORK
ACROSS CULTURES

MOVIES	SPORT	YOUTH CULTURE/ MUSIC

PARENTAL LOVE	FRIENDSHIP/ LOYALTY	SEX/ ROMANCE

Hollywood and Bollywood movies are watched by billions of people across the globe. Major sporting events such as the FIFA World Cup and the Olympics offer efficient ways to reach a global audience (see Section 3.2). Youth culture and music also tend to work well across country borders. Likewise, the themes of looking after your family, cherishing your friends, sexual attraction and romance are universally recognized. This is why global brands often look for ways to leverage these themes in their advertising, sponsorship and product placement partnerships.

With these considerations in mind, international brand teams need to decide how they should develop advertising.

MODELS FOR INTERNATIONAL
ADVERTISING DEVELOPMENT

CENTRAL DEVELOPMENT

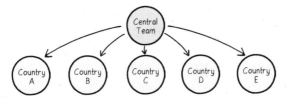

HUB DEVELOPMENT

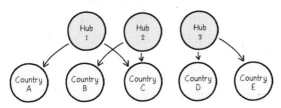

LOCAL DEVELOPMENT

CENTRAL DEVELOPMENT

In this model, the central team develops a 'tool kit' designed to equip and inspire country teams to produce brilliant local advertising. The tool kit includes:

- Brand identity rules (e.g., logos, colours, fonts, taglines, etc. and when/how to use them)
- A brand idea and/or a creative idea (see Section 5.1); all countries are expected to base their advertising on these
- Examples of creative assets such as video ad(s), video footage or static ads or imagery, which have usually been researched in a diverse set of countries and optimized; they should be used as the basis for local executions (e.g., in small countries) or act as inspiration for local content (e.g., in big countries)
- Suggestions for media combinations and activation concepts that could work well

Local marketing teams are responsible for adopting and adapting the ideas and content to produce advertising that works well in their country. They need to:

- Create the local media plan and negotiate with/buy the media (apart from any global deals with media companies such as Facebook and Google)
- Choose assets to be used as the basis for local executions
- Adapt these assets to produce executions that use the local language, feature local packaging, are consistent with local laws and are formatted for local media channels
- Create additional content (e.g., for local social media) that resonates with the local audience

You should consider a centralized ad development approach if:
- Consumers think about and use the category in a similar way across countries
- Your product portfolio and launch strategies are aligned across countries
- Perceptions of your brand are similar everywhere
- The competitive environments are broadly consistent
- Advertising that leverages global themes would work well for your brand

To make this model work for your organization, be clear on who is responsible for what, and allocate budgets accordingly. Ensure the central team has a good understanding of all the markets and cultures in which your brand operates.

HUB DEVELOPMENT

This approach is worth considering if the opportunities for central development described above exist, but only if countries are put into groups ('hubs'), rather than being lumped together. In this model, a select few countries that are most valuable for the brand are given responsibility, and budget, for developing advertising that will work well for their market and for other, broadly similar markets. There are very few global brands that develop advertising centrally that will work in every country, even allowing for localization. The Hub approach may be more practical. Global companies tend to operate at least three hubs. They might have a hub for North America/Northern Europe, one for South America/Southern Europe one for South Asia/Southeast Asia. Grouping countries into hubs should be based on these factors:
- How the category is used
- The brand's history and status in each country

- The competitive environment
- Consumer trends that might affect the brand's prospects
- The regional organization of the company

In 1954, cigarette manufacturer Marlboro developed advertising that featured the 'Marlboro Man.' He was a cowboy who represented an ideal of manhood at the time: muscular, rugged and aloof. In Asia, however, the American cowboy archetype meant very little. The approach was adapted to focus on racing drivers instead of a cowboy because in Asia, they represented the epitome of masculinity, cool and bravery.

THE MARLBORO MAN

WESTERN MARKETS   ASIAN MARKETS

LOCAL DEVELOPMENT

Local advertising development may be the best option if there is very little common ground between countries. This is rare for any brand that is marketed internationally – after all, the benefit of an international brand should be that it delivers cost efficiencies by operating across country boundaries.

In this scenario, each market has its own budget to develop advertising. Inevitably, local budgets are small. If an international brand decides to operate in this way, it can still create an advantage over local competitors if countries share their most effective ideas and content so that other markets can replicate their success. In reality, this rarely happens because each country believes their market context is unique and their customers respond to advertising in a different way. This may be true for certain brands but in many instances, the needs, priorities and advertising response are remarkably similar across countries. If this is the case, an international marketing approach is a good option but only if all key countries are persuaded to help make the platform a success.

Hybrid models are also possible. For example, a few large markets might develop their own advertising, leaving the central team to cater for all the smaller markets. This allows markets with lots of resources to produce advertising optimized for their market while enabling smaller markets to benefit from being part of a large organization with centralized resources.

5.4 THE POWER OF STORIES

When people talk about storytelling in advertising, they mean capturing the audience's attention and creating a lasting memory that's connected with the brand. Storytelling is at the heart of brand building (see Section 1.3).

A story is a sequence of events that happened in the past. A good story leaves people with something of value that might inform their future decisions and actions. In *The Storytelling Animal: How Stories Make Us Human*, Jonathan Gottschall explains how storytelling has helped humankind transfer knowledge across generations, learn from its mistakes and accumulate knowledge. Delivering information within a story makes it easier to understand, more believable and more likely to be acted upon.

Great advertising leverages the art of storytelling.

IKEA BILLBOARD AD

Numerous academic studies have demonstrated how storytelling enhances ad effectiveness. Zatwarnicka-Madura and Nowacki (2018) found that story ads are more memorable, convey higher quality perceptions and result in stronger purchase intent.

What makes a great story? To answer this question, Quesenberry and Coolsen (2014) analysed 108 Super Bowl commercials. They concluded that ads performed better if they featured more of the five stages that Shakespeare used to structure his plays.

SHAKESPEARE'S FIVE ACT STRUCTURE

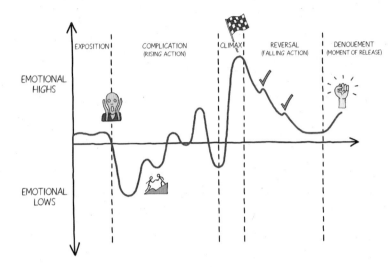

EXPOSITION

This involves setting the scene, introducing the characters, and establishing the idea that life is good and worth protecting.

COMPLICATION

A problem emerges. Something that will upset the status quo and may ruin everything. The hero of the story, given hope and the promise of support from a wise person, then rises to several challenges to address the problem.

CLIMAX

Everything culminates in one last, difficult trial. Once overcome, this solves the problem once and for all (or until the sequel).

REVERSAL

Everything goes back to normal. The status quo is restored.

DENOUEMENT

A moment to celebrate. The happy ending.

This structure is also referred to as the 'Hero's Journey': the emotional rollercoaster it creates holds people's attention and makes an ad memorable. However, telling a powerful story isn't enough. For the ad to be effective, the brand needs to play a clear role in the story so that memories from the ad are connected with the brand. Ideally, the brand plays the role of the 'wise person' who helps the consumer (the 'hero') to achieve what they want to achieve.

Znanewitz and Gilch (2016), identified six criteria for effective storytelling in advertising.

CRITERIA FOR EFFECTIVE BRAND STORYTELLING

ENGAGING

Entertaining or interesting for the target audience

BRAND-LINKED

Easy for consumers to connect the story with the brand

AUTHENTIC

Consistent with the brand's delivery, history and values

DISTINCTIVE

Unlike the stories told by other brands

STRAIGHT-FORWARD

Easy to describe in a sentence or two

SPARSE

An outline that allows people to add details using their imagination

The most effective storytelling ads tell a story that's based on the brand's strengths, engages the target audience, makes it easy for people to register the brand, is different from competitors' stories and provides enough detail for people to understand the gist of the story but allows them to fill in the gaps using their own imagination.

UK department store John Lewis is famous for telling memorable stories during the festive period. Its Christmas campaigns since 2007 have been extremely popular and effective. The heartwarming stories remind us of the value of human connection and inspire us to do our best. Advertising that speaks to us in this way tends to affect our thinking (and brand preferences) for years. Most ads are forgotten within minutes.

5.5 THE POWER OF HUMOUR

Humour is one of the most effective ways to create advertising effectiveness. Eisend (2009) found that the moment when people understand the humour (e.g., get the joke) creates a rewarding feeling which makes the moment memorable. If the brand relates to this moment, people feel more positive towards it and more likely to buy it. If the humorous idea is appealing enough, it might even be adopted into culture. For example, the phrase 'Simples' became widespread in the UK because of a series of humorous ads by Comparethemarket.com featuring a fictional meerkat community.

THE POWER OF HUMOUR IN ADVERTISING

MEMORABILITY

FEEL-GOOD FACTOR

PURCHASE INTENT

CULTURAL ADOPTION

Many leading brands leverage humour in their advertising, including Budweiser, Skittles, Fedex and Taco Bell. Humour is less commonly used in certain categories such as financial services, presumably because of fears that it might undermine perceptions of trust and professionalism. However, there have been countless successful campaigns in these categories over the years. In the 1980s, Barclaycard advertising in the UK featured a bumbling detective played by Rowan Atkinson. Insurance companies Geico and Progressive are also famous for their light-hearted campaigns. Legal service providers such as Farewill and LegalZoom have even used gentle humour in their advertising for will-writing to make the process feel less daunting.

Despite the benefits, the use of humour in advertising has declined over the past 20 years. According to research company Kantar Millward Brown, the proportion of ads leveraging humour in 2021 was just 33% compared to 54% in 2000. A possible reason for this is that humour doesn't always travel well, making it a risky approach for brands developing advertising internationally. Humour is often culture specific. Styles of humour that work well in one country can fall flat in others. Sarcasm, mockery, schadenfreude, dark humour, zaniness and wordplay are often lost in translation. Like in the world of film and television, physical comedy and visual gags have a better chance of working well in multiple countries. The snacks brand Doritos is famous for using slapstick comedy in its advertising to great effect. Volkswagen and IKEA are known for their clever visual gags.

IKEA AD

USING CELEBRITIES

Using a celebrity to promote your brand is a tempting idea. The partnership between Nespresso and George Clooney, after all, is widely regarded as world class marketing. Clooney is well known and admired by billions of people. When he comes on screen, people pay attention. He is seen as discerning, sophisticated, cool and sexy. These positive associations shape how people think of Nespresso. Also, because we have seen and read so much about George, we feel that we know him. We trust what he says as if he were our friend – an effect caused by what is known in psychology as 'parasocial interaction.'

THE TEMPTATION TO USE A CELEBRITY

ATTENTION

POSITIVE ASSOCIATIONS

CREDIBILITY

According to Sliburyte (2009), however, academic evidence about the effectiveness of using celebrities in advertising is mixed. Positive effects have been observed, but there are several downsides. There is a risk that the celebrity will steal the show (it's their job, after all), overshadowing the brand and resulting in advertising with little commercial impact. This, combined with the high cost, lack of exclusivity and possibility that the celebrity could desert the brand at any time, means that using a celebrity is rarely a risk worth taking.

ARE CELEBRITIES WORTH IT?

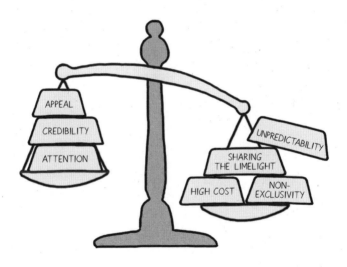

There have even been cases when a celebrity has tarnished the reputation of their sponsor.

For example, in 2014, LeBron James tweeted that his Samsung Galaxy Note 3 had lost all his data, despite the fact that he had backed it up. He also tweeted that he was switching back to an iPhone. This incident caused some embarrassment for Samsung, as James was a brand ambassador for the company at the time.

Some brands have invested heavily to secure a long-term partnership with a celebrity so that they become a distinctive brand asset (See Chapter 6). The drawback of this strategy is that when the deal finally runs its course, the 'asset' cannot be used again. The brand must start from scratch with a replacement and invest all over again to build a strong connection between the asset and the brand. You are better off inventing a brand character (see Section 6.3). They will work for free, be unique to your brand and remain loyal forever.

PRODUCT DEMOS

According to advertising research company Kantar Millward Brown, three quarters of ads in their database show the product being used, how it works, how it is made or the benefits it delivers. These ads tend to outperform the 25% of ads that don't feature the product overtly.

One of the major benefits of including a product demo in your advertising is that it helps ensure people register your brand's name. However, simply featuring your product in your advertising is no guarantee of success. Ad effectiveness depends on how well the demo is integrated into the narrative and whether it is done with imagination and originality. A predictable, boring demo sequence spliced into an otherwise interesting ad can even disengage the audience and reduce the ad's memorability.

Generally speaking, product demos are most powerful if your product has a genuine, tangible, functional advantage over your competitors. At the time of writing, Google recently introduced a mobile phone with a unique feature – the ability to transfer battery power to other phones. Its advertising is centred on this advantage and demonstrates clearly how it works. The advertising has performed brilliantly in pre-testing. Even if your brand's strengths aren't unique, demonstrating them might still be a powerful advertising approach. Here are different ways to leverage product demonstrations in advertising.

ROLES PRODUCT DEMOS CAN PLAY

THE
UNFAMILIAR

PROVE COMPETITIVE
SUPERIORITY

VISUALIZE UNSEEN
FEATURES/BENEFITS

DRAMATIZE
A STRENGTH

CONVEY PRODUCT'S
ACTION VIA METAPHOR

DEMYSTIFY THE UNFAMILIAR

People are reluctant to buy a product if they are unsure how it works or how they'd use it. Brands introducing new business models, categories or novel ways of using existing products can use advertising to educate consumers. By showing how the product works, the advertising makes people more comfortable with the idea of trying something new. It reduces the risk factor that might otherwise have prevented them from considering the brand.

When Cazoo launched in the UK in 2018, it represented a revolutionary way to buy a used car. Customers choose from a wide selection of cars on the brand's website. Once purchased, the car is delivered to their door. If the customer is not happy with the car for any reason, they can return it within seven days without penalty. Cazoo won a Silver IPA Effectiveness Award in 2022 for its advertising. The campaign explained the purchase process and reassured customers who may have been too nervous to buy a car without seeing it or taking a test drive.

PROVE COMPETITIVE SUPERIORITY

If your product is genuinely superior to your competitors and you have a convincing way to prove it, you should consider communicating this through advertising. Pepsi found that in blind taste tests involving a few sips, their brand was preferred to Coke. They highlighted this through a series of ads during the 1980s.

Advertising for kitchen paper brand Plenty has featured a Spanish character called 'Juan Sheet' who uses just 'one sheet' of Plenty to mop up a spill that would cause inferior kitchen papers to disintegrate.

Duracell wasn't the first alkaline battery available in the UK, but it was the first to demonstrate their superiority over traditional carbon batteries. They did this using a TV ad in 1973 featuring a fluffy, pink, battery-powered rabbit toy that played a drum. The toy powered by Duracell kept going six times longer than several identical toys foolishly relying on carbon batteries. Duracell's competitor, Energizer, later acquired the rights to use the bunny in its North American advertising.

VISUALIZE UNSEEN FEATURES/BENEFITS

Product demonstrations are particularly powerful for brands whose advantages are normally invisible to the consumer. Household appliance manufacturer Dyson sells products that are functionally superior to competitors thanks to its unique technology. Dyson uses stylish visualizations to show what's special about its technology to help convince consumers that its products are worth paying more for.

For many years, Dove cleansing bar was unique because ¼ of its ingredients comprised moisturizing cream. The brand used an animated sequence in its advertising showing the moisturizer being poured into the bar to help people remember what made the brand special.

Cadbury Dairy Milk chocolate uses something similar. The Second World War resulted in food rationing in the UK between 1940 and 1954. Cadbury's promise of providing nutrition from cocoa fats, sugar and milk was highly relevant during this period. The healthiness of milk has remained a component of the brand's identity ever since. The brand still talks about containing 'a glass and a half of fresh milk in every half pound' and uses a visual to reinforce this message in its advertising and on its packaging.

DRAMATIZE A STRENGTH

Advertising can take a strength of the brand, and make it seem important. The trick is to make the advantage tangible and easy to imagine. This technique is widely used and effective.

In 1886, Levi's introduced a logo featuring two horses trying to pull apart a pair of Levi's jeans. It was designed to symbolize the strength and robustness of their jeans. Other advertisers have successfully brought the strengths of their brand to life in similar ways. In 1978, wallpaper adhesive brand Solvite stuck a man to a panel via his overalls before using a helicopter to lift the panel and fly it with the man still attached. More recently Mous, a brand of durable cases for smartphones and tablets, produced a series of videos for social media and TV to dramatize the damage protection provided by their products. In their first TV ad, 50 passers-by were given Mous cases for their phones, which were filmed being thrown high up and landing on hard paving. None of the phones were damaged – to the relief of the participants and delight of the advertiser.

CONVEY PRODUCT'S ACTION VIA METAPHOR

Metaphors are a great way to communicate your brand's benefit in a memorable way. UK breakfast cereal Ready Brek grew rapidly during the 1970s and 80s thanks to its campaign known as 'Central Heating for Kids.' In the ads, children who had eaten Ready Brek porridge in the morning are shown having an orange glow around them, keeping them warm as they walk to school in the cold. Several pharmaceutical brands have developed their own visual metaphors to bring the benefits of their products alive in their advertising. Gaviscon advertising, for example, shows miniature cartoon firemen hosing the product in the oesophagus and stomach of a heartburn sufferer, alleviating the pain.

CHAPTER 6

DISTINCTIVE
BRAND ASSETS

6.1 WHY DISTINCTIVE BRAND ASSETS ARE VALUABLE

Distinctive brand assets are any images, characters, logos, shapes, rituals, typefaces, words or sounds that come to mind when people think about your brand.

DISTINCTIVE ASSETS EXAMPLES

IMAGES

CHARACTERS/ CELEBRITIES

LOGOS

SHAPES

RITUALS

TYPEFACES

WORDS

JUST DO IT.

SOUNDS/ MUSIC

These assets are evoked in people's minds either when they spontaneously think about the brand or if they come across the brand and are triggered to think about it. The benefit of these assets coming to mind is that they can result in strong memories and feelings. These dominate the consumer's thoughts for a couple of seconds, making them more likely to buy the brand. The brand-building role of advertising is to build these mental associations over time. The activation role of advertising is to trigger these associations just before the purchase decision is made. Featuring the same distinctive brand assets makes both forms of advertising more effective.

Evidence for the benefit of developing distinctive brand assets is strong. In *Building Distinctive Brand Assets* (2018), Jenni Romaniuk shows that brands with strong distinctive assets have higher ad awareness, better brand recall and stronger purchase intentions compared to brands without distinctive assets.

6.2 WHICH BRAND ASSETS TO INVEST IN

Jenni Romaniuk has proposed a 2x2 matrix to help brands identify which assets to build over time via advertising investment. Here's what the matrix might look like for 'Brand UK.'

DISTINCTIVE BRAND ASSETS GRID EXAMPLES

STRONGLY ASSOCIATED with brand

WEAKLY ASSOCIATED with brand

ASSOCIATED WITH OTHER BRANDS (TOO)

UNIQUE

Looking at the quadrant in the bottom left, the UK has some connection with artistic and maritime traditions – but many other countries have even stronger associations with these areas, so the opportunity to create a distinctive brand asset based on them is limited. Moving up, the UK has a strong association with sports such as soccer, rugby and cricket, but these are not unique. Other countries are also associated with these sports such as Germany, Ireland and India. The properties in the top right quadrant are most important to Brand UK. These are strongly associated with the country and are not linked with other countries.

Brands that haven't yet built a strong set of distinctive assets should look at properties within the bottom-right quadrant. This quadrant may provide opportunities to establish unique assets. Brand UK has plenty of assets in the top right quadrant, so it doesn't need to build new ones.

6.3 VISUAL STYLES

Trying to create a distinctive brand asset by owning a particular visual style is a tall order. To succeed, the visual style must be truly unique, and the brand must use it consistently across channels and over time.

Here are some examples of brands that have built a strong association with a particular look:

- Tiffany – monochrome apart from its iconic Tiffany Blue colour (Pantone 1837)
- Google – the three primary colours + green on a white background
- Guinness – mainly dark hues with cream and a hint of gold, reflecting the drink and its logo
- Tim Burton movies – the gothic style and doll-like figures with large eyes

The problem with using a visual style as a distinctive brand asset is that the style could be copied. Calvin Klein's photographic style has been replicated by many other brands. The photographer responsible for some of the brand's iconic advertising in the 1980s, Bruce Weber, has since worked with Ralph Lauren, Abercrombie & Fitch, and Versace.

DISTINCTIVE VISUAL STYLE

ABSOLUT VODKA

LEGO

TARGET

APPLE IPOD

RED BULL

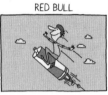

A better bet in the long term is to combine a unique visual style with something owned by your brand. Absolut Vodka, LEGO and Red Bull feature their products; Target highlights its logo. Apple's famous iPod advertising featured their iconic earbuds.

6.4 BRAND CHARACTERS

Inventing a brand character and using it consistently across touchpoints and over time is a highly effective way to build a brand's mental availability. As mentioned in Section 5.6, brand characters have many advantages over celebrities. They don't demand high fees, are available when you need them and are exclusive to your brand. Brand characters can be the common thread that links all the brand's communications together in people's minds. If brand characters come to consumers' minds close to the moment of purchase (e.g., because they are featured in point-of-sale activity), they can influence purchase decisions by triggering brand memories.

Brand characters can take any form. They could be based on real people such as Colonel Sanders. They could be fictional humans such as Ronald McDonald or 'The Most Interesting Man in the World,' who features in the advertising for lager brand Dos Equis. Animals are also popular choices. Many are anthropomorphic creations such as Kellogg's Frosties' Tony the Tiger. Others, such as the duck used by the insurance company Aflac, behave naturalistically. Some of the most successful brand characters are manifestations of the product itself. Planter's Mr. Peanut, the M&M characters, the Michelin Man, and the Pillsbury Doughboy are all well-known examples.

BRAND CHARACTER EXAMPLES

Successful characters move with the times. The character on the left of the illustration is the Amul girl, who has been the mascot for an Indian dairy brand since 1966. She became famous thanks to her cheeky and independent spirit, which captured the hearts of Indian housewives. In line with changing societal attitudes, the Amul Girl has been portrayed in ways that celebrate women's achievements and empowerment, including references to women breaking barriers in various fields.

When it comes to international advertising, fictional characters living in a fantasy world have an advantage. People from countries all over the world can identify with worlds and characters from a different universe. The global popularity of sci-fi and fantasy movies reflects this. In advertising, showing a real Japanese family enjoying breakfast will resonate with someone from Kyoto but may feel remote and irrelevant to someone in the American Midwest. Imaginary worlds can transcend cultures and enable advertisers to connect with audiences across the globe. From 2000, Unilever's fabric conditioner brand Comfort used an advertising campaign featuring animated characters made of cloth. The original ads were produced by Aardman, the Oscar-winning animation studio responsible for the Wallace and Gromit series. The campaign appealed to consumers in Europe, Asia and beyond.

COMFORT CLOTH WORLD

Characters can become associated with a brand through their voice alone. In the UK, Dexter Fletcher, a star from Guy Ritchie's movie *Lock, Stock and Two Smoking Barrels*, has provided voiceovers for McDonald's ads for many years and comedian Lenny Henry has provided the voiceover for advertising from UK hotel chain Premier Inn since 2008.

6.5 TAGLINES

A tagline (or brand line, slogan, catchphrase, motto, jingle) can serve two purposes. It can help consumers makes sense of and remember the advertising they have just seen, and it can become a distinctive brand asset in its own right.

Many of the world's most successful brands have memorable taglines. Here are a few examples.

- Nike – Just Do It
- Kit Kat – Have a Break, Have a Kit Kat
- M&Ms – Melts in your mouth, not in your hands
- BMW – The Ultimate Driving Machine
- American Express – Don't leave home without it
- Apple – Think Different
- KFC – Finger Lickin' Good
- McDonald's – I'm Lovin' It

The effectiveness of taglines is highly variable. For every hit there are countless others that time has long forgotten. Tagline failures occur because the brand team hasn't found the right one, hasn't integrated it into their communications effectively or hasn't invested enough to establish it. For a tagline to work, it needs to come to mind when people are thinking about the brand and/or buying the category. Ideally, it needs to become famous.

WHAT MAKES A TAGLINE EFFECTIVE

MNEMONIC
for the meaning of the ad and brand

APPEALING
so people want to remember it

CONSISTENT
across media and over time

MNEMONIC

A tagline is remembered if it completes or builds on the ad's story or encapsulates the ad's meaning. An effective tagline acts as shorthand for what the brand is all about. This influences people when they are choosing which brand to buy.

APPEALING

This is where artistry is key. Taglines can be appealing for many reasons. Being distinctive, unexpected or inspirational can work well. So can humour, rhythm, rhyme, sound effects or a tune. The best taglines capture the public's imagination and are adopted into everyday language. Simples!

CONSISTENT

Repetition helps a tagline to be remembered and become strongly associated with the brand in consumers' minds. The association may build faster if the brand name is an essential part of the tagline. If the link becomes strong, the tagline can influence purchase decisions for years. Kit Kat has used variations of the same tagline for nearly a century.

KIT KAT AD FROM 1939

Taglines with a musical component can become exceptionally memorable. At the time of writing, UK primary school children across the country are singing 'I sold my car, to We Buy Any Car' in the playground. Taglines set to music can become powerful earworms. Here are just a few examples:

- Just Eat – Did somebody say Just Eat?
- Maybelline – Maybe she's born with it … maybe it's Maybelline!
- Mars – A Mars a Day Helps You Work, Rest and Play
- Heinz Baked Beans – Beanz Meanz Heinz!
- Bodyform sanitary towels – Whoooa Bodyform, Bodyformed for you

6.6 SOUND AND MUSIC

Having a tuneful tagline or jingle is only one way sound and music can be used to create distinctive brand assets. A brand can build an asset from any distinctive sounds it uses repeatedly. Sound logos (or audio signatures) are tunes or sounds that have become part of a brand's identity. Here are some famous examples:

FAMILYMART
Shoppers entering a FamilyMart convenience store in Japan, the Philippines, Thailand, Taiwan and parts of mainland China will always hear the same 12-note sequence.

MGM
The sound of a lion roaring has been used since the studio's first movie with sound in 1928. Other studios including 20th Century Fox, Disney and Marvel also have distinctive sounds that they use at the start of all their movies.

INTEL
The chip manufacturer has used its famous 'Bong' as its sonic signature since 1994.

MCDONALD'S

Their tagline, 'I'm Lovin' It,' is usually accompanied by a five-note sequence which has become an asset in its own right. It comes from a song commissioned by McDonald's, written by Pharrell Williams (and others) and recorded as a single by Justin Timberlake in 2003.

DOMINO'S

In 2021, the pizza company created an app for easy group orders and used an ad featuring yodelling to promote it. The sound 'Domin-oh-hoo-hoo' has since become one of the brand's strongest and distinctive assets and is used in most of its ads.

Some brands have gone further by linking their brand with whole pieces of music or musical genres.

AIRTEL

The Indian communications provider has used the same tune, composed by award-winning musician A.R. Rahman, since 2002. It has become the most downloaded ringtone on the planet.

EL ALMENDRO

The Spanish confection brand uses traditional, nostalgic Spanish music and songs in its advertising.

BRITISH AIRWAYS

BA plays 'Flower Duet' by Léo Delibes from the opera *Lakmé* in its aeroplanes and has featured it in many of its ads. The connection with this classical piece reinforces the brand's quality perceptions and helps customers feel calm and relaxed.

JET2HOLIDAYS

Since 2015, 'Hold My Hand' by Jess Glynne has been used by Jet2holidays on their TV ads. The catchy tune works with the visuals to convey family togetherness, and these have both become strongly linked with the brand.

GO COMPARE

The insurance company has featured a fictional opera singer called 'Gio Compario' in its advertising since 2009. He sings about the brand's features and benefits, ending each ad with a musical crescendo and the words 'You'll thank your stars that you went with Go Compare!' (or similar).

GO COMPARE MASCOT GIO COMPARIO

There have also been cases of single tracks used in one-off ads that have become strongly linked with the brand. 'I'd Like to Teach the World to Sing (In Perfect Harmony)' is a song originally created for a Coca-Cola ad in 1971 and later released as a full-length song. It captured the mood of a generation and is still associated with the brand to this day. Australian department store The Good Guys used a version of 'Good Vibrations' by The Beach Boys. Levi's jeans used a string of songs in the 1980s and 1990s and is still linked in many people's minds with 'I Heard it on the Grapevine' by Marvin Gaye and 'Inside' by Stiltskin.

6.7 BRAND RITUALS

Developing a ritual around how your brand is used can enhance the brand's memorability. Advertising can be used to raise awareness of a brand's ritual and help it catch on. The goal is to make the ritual famous and turn it into a cultural phenomenon.

OREOS

Oreos has created ads showing how its cookies are supposed to be eaten for several decades. An ad from 1990 showed a toddler being guided by his dad on how to twist the cookie apart, lick the cream, and dunk the cookie into a glass of milk. The jingle accompanying the very first ad in this series went, 'Sometimes I pull them apart and sometimes I just eat it, but O-R-E-O, how do you eat it?' The twist-lick-dunk ritual has featured in many of the brand's campaigns since then, catching on in countries around the world.

KIT KAT

The ritual of taking a break, snapping off one the product's fingers and then snapping it in half, has been featured in Kit Kat's advertising for over 80 years. The ritual has been the core idea behind hundreds of outdoor, print, TV and digital ads, helping the brand come to mind when people need a break.

KIT KAT SNAP RITUAL

GUINNESS

Guinness is perhaps the best example of a brand that has created a ritual to make the brand memorable and appealing. Here are some of the rituals that Diageo, the company that owns Guinness, have associated with the idea of serving the perfect pint of Guinness:

1. Use a cool, clean, dry glass
2. Grip it at the base
3. Hold it at a 45° angle to the tap
4. Pour the beer slowly down the side of the glass
5. Let it settle for at least 2 minutes before serving

The whole process takes at least 3 minutes. This could have been seen by consumers as an inconvenience, but Guinness turned it into a benefit through its advertising reminding us that 'good things come to those who wait.' The UK TV ad *Anticipation* is a great example of how Guinness made itself famous and appealing by focusing on the unusually long time required for the beer to be served. The campaign has become so famous that it has sparked numerous homages. The ad below was produced by a creative who didn't work for the brand but wanted to pay tribute to the brilliant idea behind much of the brand's advertising. This unofficial ad was shared on social media in 2023 when Prince Charles finally became King of the United Kingdom, having waited for over 70 years for his chance to wear the crown.

GUINNNESS CHARLES III AD HOMAGE

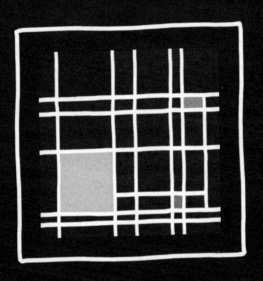

CHAPTER 7

STATIC
VISUAL ADS

7.1 GRABBING ATTENTION WITHIN TWO SECONDS

Ads using static visuals appear in newspapers, magazines, posters, billboards, social media feeds, websites and apps. To be effective, they need to be visually arresting and interesting. They must grab and hold the consumer's attention within a second or two. Otherwise, the viewer will quickly turn the page, look elsewhere, or scroll further down their feed.

SOCIAL MEDIA AD EXPOSURE

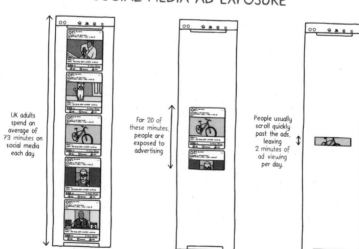

UK adults spend an average of 73 minutes on social media each day

For 20 of these minutes, people are exposed to advertising

People usually scroll quickly past the ads, leaving 2 minutes of ad viewing per day.

On average, people spend only about one and a half seconds looking at static visual ads in social, print, outdoor and digital media (see Section 8.2). That's roughly how long it takes to glance at your watch. One way to make your static ad effective is to convey the brand and message quickly, before people inevitably move on. Alternatively, you could make your ad remarkable enough to hold people's attention for longer than typical ads, providing the opportunity to forge more powerful, long-lasting brand memories.

There is no formula for creating an ad that's guaranteed to grab people's attention. Creativity is the key. However, when reviewing advertising concepts, it is worth bearing in mind what helps an ad command attention through its visuals. Here are some of those key characteristics:

HOW TO GRAB VISUAL ATTENTION

ORIGINALITY

INTRIGUE

VISUAL CLARITY

EMOTION

DIRECT GAZE

PERSONAL RESONANCE

ORIGINALITY

People pay more attention to things they have never seen before. Originality is key to advertising effectiveness.

INTRIGUE

Unusual, unexpected imagery or text makes people curious to understand what they are seeing. This makes them spend longer looking at the ad trying to figure it out. Visual metaphors tend to be effective (see Section 7.3). Posing a question in the ad's headline can also work well because our brains are hard-wired to try to think of an answer. Generating intrigue ensures viewers spend at least some mental energy processing your advertising.

VISUAL CLARITY

People's attention is drawn to imagery that is clear and stands out from our visually complex world. Using uncluttered designs, minimal words and strong, contrasting colours can help.

EMOTION

Showing emotionally charged imagery helps an ad get noticed. This is why so many ads feature cute babies, cuddly animals or gorgeous people. These elements are so common, in fact, that ads using them might be ignored due to their lack of originality. Controversial or shocking imagery also provokes an emotional response and can be highly effective in advertising, if used with thought and sensitivity.

DIRECT GAZE

If a person depicted in an ad looks directly at the viewer, the viewer can't help but have their emotions stirred. This is known as the gaze induction effect. It is an effective technique for drawing people into an ad.

PERSONAL RESONANCE

In the same way as we pick out our name being mentioned at a noisy gathering, we are attuned to notice any visual elements or words that personally resonate. Showing things that many of the target audience can immediately identify with is a good way to grab attention. If technology allows the advertising to be personalized to individual viewers, this could take its impact to the next level, but care must be taken not to violate people's privacy.

The trick is to harness the attention gained in these ways (and many others) while ensuring viewers register the brand and remember positive, relevant things about it.

7.2 DIRECTING WHERE PEOPLE LOOK

The composition of an ad plays a vital role in determining which parts of the ad people look at. Advertisers need to leverage the principles of visual design to direct people's attention.

When we look at a static visual, our eyes are drawn, initially, to its 'dominant element' – whatever stands out most from the rest of the image. This could be its size, colour, shape, texture, brightness, sharpness, etc. The image below was inspired by the great Dutch artist Piet Mondrian. When people look at this image, their attention is initially drawn to the large, shaded square. Their eyes are then directed to the two smaller shaded squares – the secondary and tertiary focal points within the image.

HOW TO DIRECT VISUAL ATTENTION

In real life, whether the viewer can be bothered to spend more time looking at an ad depends on how much interest its dominant element generates and whether the ad has any secondary elements that also stand out from the background. Effective ads convey their message and connect it with the brand before people get bored with what they're seeing and move on.

You may have come across the 'Z' or 'F' patterns used to describe how people's eyes move as they look at a screen. However, these are based primarily on how people look at blocks of text, rather than creative images. The 'Rule of Thirds', 'Golden Triangle', 'Fibonacci Spiral' and 'Golden Ratio' are all useful concepts for composing an attractive, well-balanced image, but they all pale into insignificance compared to the principles of visual hierarchy, focal points and flow described above.

The image below summarizes the principles you need to apply in order to produce an effective static visual ad. The word 'Thirsty' is designed to stand out and grab attention by using an unusual typeface, a large font and a colour that contrasts with the background. The sunrays then direct viewers' attention to the secondary focal point, which is the brand (i.e., the thing that provides a solution to the 'thirsty' consumer need).

STATIC VISUAL AD ILLUSTRATION

The questions you need to ask yourself when developing a static visual ad are:

- Is the overall aesthetic compelling enough to draw people's attention?
- Which element is dominant, i.e., what will people look at first?
- Will this create enough interest/intrigue to make people spend time looking at the ad?
- What will they look at next?
- Will most viewers register the brand and key message before losing interest in the ad?

7.3 THE POWER OF VISUAL METAPHORS

In today's cluttered media environment, an ad needs to convey the brand and what it wants people to remember about it within a few seconds (see Section 7.1). One of the best ways of doing this is to use a visual metaphor. Numerous academic studies including McQuarrie & Mick (2003) and McQuarrie & Phillips (2005), have concluded that visual metaphors enhance ad effectiveness in multiple ways:

- Create intrigue so that people stop and look at the ad
- Produce a pleasurable experience if they solve the 'puzzle'
- Make people feel positive towards the brand and more likely to buy it

Visual metaphors work well in advertising because they forge new mental connections with the brand within the 1-2 seconds most static visual ads are seen for. If the metaphor conjures the desired associations and links them with the brand, the ad has done its job before viewers look away, turn the page or continue scrolling. There is no need for them to read anything. This relies, of course, on people understanding the metaphor.

In Chapter 15 of *Persuasive Imagery: A Consumer Response Perspective*, Barbara Phillips describes how the best metaphors provide enough challenge to be interesting but not so much that viewers can't understand them within a few seconds.

THE POWER OF VISUAL METAPHORS IN ADVERTISING

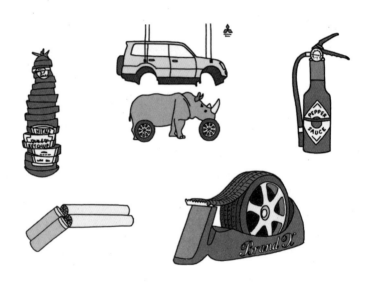

The examples on the left work well because viewers are familiar with the properties of the brand and the object it has been fused with. The pepper sauce is famous for its heat; a fire extinguisher puts out fires. The sticky tape dispenser is easily recognized due to its shape, and most people know that good tyres stick to the road.

Kim and Kim (2019) found that visual metaphors are particularly effective for brands with an established reputation and in categories consumers don't care much about. Brands people already know about and trust can use visual metaphors to provide a reminder of their strengths – there's no need to prove them. Similarly, if people aren't interested in the category, they are more likely to accept a message conveyed via a visual metaphor at face value. Low-involvement categories include utility suppliers, insurance providers, cleaning products and staple foods.

It is believed that in these scenarios there is less need for any factual substantiation of the brand benefits to be implied by the metaphor.

7.4 BRANDING FOR STATIC VISUAL ADS

Whether or not people register which brand an ad is for has a massive influence on its effectiveness. Even the most engaging creative has little impact on brand perceptions or sales if the brand isn't part of what people remember. Poor brand linkage is arguably the most common reason for weak advertising ROI.

To ensure strong brand linkage, at least one of the visual elements viewers focus on before looking away needs to trigger the brand in people's minds. This could be the product itself, its logo, or one of its distinctive brand assets (see Chapter 6).

Here are three ways to achieve strong brand linkage for static visual ads.

ACHIEVING STRONG BRANDING
FOR STATIC VISUAL ADS

PUT YOUR PRODUCT CENTRE STAGE

LEVERAGE ONE OF
YOUR DBAS

DIRECT ATTENTION TO YOUR LOGO

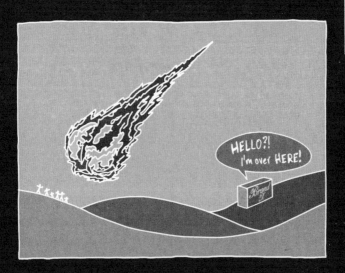

CHAPTER 8

VIDEO ADS

8.1 COMMANDING ATTENTION WITHIN SIX SECONDS

All video ads need to grab attention early and hold it for long enough for viewers to remember the brand and connect it with the desired associations. TV ads must stop people from picking up a magazine, checking their phone, or going off to make a cup of tea during the ad break. Skippable YouTube ads need to be enticing enough within the first six seconds to prevent the viewer from clicking through to start watching their chosen video. Videos on social media must work even faster.

According to a report by media analysis company Ebiquity (2021), the average viewing time on Facebook is just 1.6 seconds. People scroll straight past most ads (see: https://ebiquity.com/news-in-sights/research/the-challenge-of-attention/).

AVERAGE EYES-ON DWELL TIME BY MEDIUM

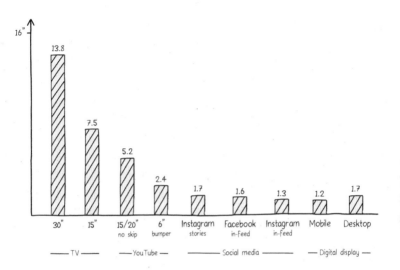

So, how can an ad be designed so that it grabs people's attention within the first few seconds and makes people want to watch more?

VISUAL HOOKS

If your video includes a striking visual or two within the first few seconds, it will help draw viewers in. Powerful, interesting visuals at the start are essential for channels such as Facebook, that people usually experience with the sound off (see Section 8.3). The principles described for static visuals in Section 7.1 apply equally well here. Attention is gained through visuals that are clear and bold, original, unusual, intriguing, emotionally charged or personally resonant.

COMMANDING ATTENTION WITH VIDEO ADS

VISUAL HOOKS

AUDIO HOOKS

| CLEAN & BOLD | ORIGINAL/ UNUSUAL/ INTRIGUING | EMOTIONAL/ RESONANT | HIGHER PITCH | RISING PITCH | FAMILIAR INTERVALS |

Video ads also have the opportunity to grab and hold people's attention via their audio.

AUDIO HOOKS

For any channels that are experienced unmuted, sounds can be just as effective as visuals. Just as a whistle will make any dog turn and look, certain sounds, including whistles, can be used to command human attention. In 1993, cable TV company HBO started using the 'Static Angel' sound affect at the start of all its programmes. It consists of white noise followed by a pleasing chord. It tells viewers to get ready to watch some highly engaging TV such as *The Sopranos*, *The Wire*, *Succession* and *Sex and the City*.

HIGHER PITCH

The audio backdrop of everyday life (conversation, car engines, the hum of appliances, keyboard typing), tends to be low in pitch. Shorter, sharper sounds grab our attention (doorbells, alarms, sirens, screams). This explains why higher pitch sounds at the start of video ads can be used to draw people in.

RISING PITCH

A rising pitch creates a sense of excitement and expectation. Our brains interpret this audio pattern with upward movement and progress, which makes us want to find out what will come next. It suggests the possibility of an imminent climax – something most of us would rather not miss out on.

FAMILIAR INTERVALS

People are drawn in if they hear a harmonious sound using familiar musical intervals (such as a 'perfect 5th'). Discordant sounds can also grab attention, but they tend to be unsettling and less effective at encouraging people to continue watching an ad.

Marketers should aim to entice viewers to watch an ad beyond the first few seconds. This isn't, however, always necessary. In *Making Memories*, advertising and cinematography guru Chuck Young concluded it takes only about five seconds to create a 'meaningful moment' in any form of video. This may explain why YouTube pre-roll ads can be skipped after five seconds. It is possible to tell a simple, memorable story within five seconds, but it isn't easy. In my experience, the best examples show the product itself or a distinctive brand asset (see Chapter 6) to convey the brand quickly and/or a visual metaphor to convey the meaning quickly (see Section 7.3).

With many media channels giving viewers control over how much of an ad they see, an effective strategy is to structure your video in a similar way to how newspaper editors structure their stories. Grab attention right at the start (the headline), pique people's curiosity within the next few seconds (the lead), and then deliver a memorable 15-second story – expanding it for another 10-15 seconds for anyone still watching (the body). Anyone sticking with the ad after this must be extremely interested, so give them all the details about the product's features, benefits and where to buy (the tail).

A BRAND BUILDING AD FOR THE DIGITAL AGE

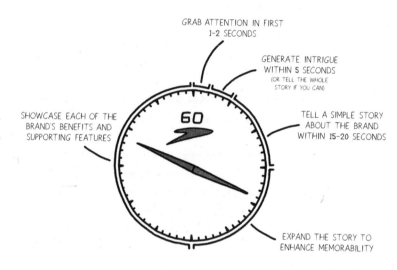

GRAB ATTENTION IN FIRST 1-2 SECONDS

GENERATE INTRIGUE WITHIN 5 SECONDS (OR TELL THE WHOLE STORY IF YOU CAN)

TELL A SIMPLE STORY ABOUT THE BRAND WITHIN 15-20 SECONDS

SHOWCASE EACH OF THE BRAND'S BENEFITS AND SUPPORTING FEATURES

EXPAND THE STORY TO ENHANCE MEMORABILITY

8.2 DIRECTING WHERE PEOPLE LOOK

The principles described in Section 7.2 for directing the eye when producing static visuals are also relevant for video ads. However, when you create moving images, there is another important consideration. At each moment, viewers have a choice of where to look – if they don't look at what you intended them to look at, it's too late. Nobody rewinds an ad. When they come across the ad again, they'll invariably focus on the same things, and miss the same things. The director and editor of the film need to control people's gaze to ensure they notice any elements that are critical to convey the ad's intended meaning and the brand role. A common error is for the video to include a moving element that distracts attention at the exact moment viewers' attention needs to be directed at the brand.

DON'T DISTRACT ATTENTION FROM YOUR BRAND

If two or more elements compete for attention at any moment in a video ad, the viewer is likely to shift their focus quickly from one to the other. This creates a sense of unease and confusion that might cause viewers to look away. If viewers do continue watching, they're unlikely to follow what's going on, and they will probably miss something important (such as the brand). Fast cutting between scenes can have the same effect, due to what's known as cognitive overload. This is particularly true for older audiences. Eye-tracking tests involving a sample of respondents, or simulated using AI, will quickly highlight these kinds of issues.

An ad's audio and visual components also need to be carefully orchestrated. If it isn't easy for people to combine them into a coherent story, they tend to focus just on the visuals, or just on the audio. The brain does this to avoid the feeling of confusion caused by cognitive dissonance. Great filmmakers, such as Disney, use sound and vision in perfect harmony so that everyone follows what's going on and experiences the intended emotional journey and meaning.

8.3 ROLE OF SOUND AND MUSIC

Music and sound play a major role in the success of video ads.

THE ROLE OF MUSIC & SOUND IN ADVERTISING

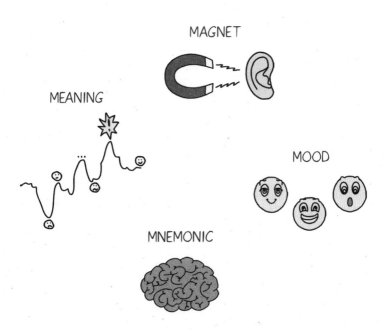

MAGNET

MEANING

MOOD

MNEMONIC

MAGNET

People can look away from a screen if they're not interested in the visuals, but music and sound in the video can gain their attention at any point. Audio techniques can be used to ensure people pay attention to pivotal moments. The audio hooks mentioned in Section 8.1 can be used to do this. Music can be used to motivate people to watch an ad through to the end. A pleasing harmony or popular piece of music make people want to hear more of the tune. Imagine hearing, "Wake me up before you go-go, ah, take me dancing tonight" and skipping the ad before hearing "I wanna hit that high, yeah, yeah!" It's practically impossible.

A musical crescendo signals that something exciting is about to happen. Revealing the message or featuring the brand when the sound reaches its peak increases the chances of viewers remembering these key elements. The sound effect, known as a 'hit' or 'slam', can also be used to emphasize important moments in an ad. A hit is a quick, loud sound – like you'd hear if you dropped a heavy book onto a solid floor. Hits are often used to signal that a character has suddenly discovered something, or to draw attention to the brand logo at the end of an ad.

MEANING

Visuals alone can tell a story, but the audio can make the meaning clearer, more powerful and more memorable. A 'whoosh' is a short sound that starts quietly, increases in volume and intensity, and then fades, like a quick rush of wind. It is used during the fight scenes of John Wick movies. A 'whoosh' reinforces the impression of movement and speed. The 'sad trombone' sound, familiar from cartoons and comedy films, is used to tell the audience that a big mistake has just occurred.

Many other sound effects are used to help viewers understand what's going on in an ad. Glass shattering, or the sound of a record being scratched, signal that something has suddenly gone wrong. Cheering, clapping or church bells are used to signify success or celebration. A clock ticking conveys that time is passing. These conventions are engrained in our psyche because they have been used so often in the films and television we have watched since childhood. They act as a universal language that ad makers can exploit to tell clear, memorable stories in a short space of time.

Financial services company Mastercard uses sound design in a creative and thoughtful way. It cues various needs and occasions that have become associated with the brand. In addition to the 'Mastercard Melody' that plays at the end of every ad, their ads use carefully selected soundscapes and music to enhance storytelling and evoke specific emotions. The brand's audio choices fit the narrative and visual elements in their ads perfectly to create a cohesive experience. Mastercard uses the same sound logo and audio cues in its mobile apps, websites and digital payment interactions.

MOOD

Music has a major influence on the mood created by an ad and whether it conveys the desired ideas and feelings. Tempo, rhythm, instrumentation and musical genre all have an impact. Fast-paced, high-energy music evokes excitement and urgency. Slower, ambient music creates a more relaxed and contemplative atmosphere. A soft piano melody tends to generate a sentimental or nostalgic mood. Rock music can convey energy, excitement and the spirit of rebellion. Pop music is more about levity, fun and happiness. Classical music lends an air of sophistication and elegance.

Sound effects also play a role in developing the mood of an ad as the story develops. The slow tolling of a bell creates a feeling of sobriety. Birds chirping conveys peace and tranquillity. The sound of thunder conjures a sense of nervous suspense.

MNEMONIC

Sounds and music can become effective brand mnemonics that boost your brand's memorability and make it easier for future ads to be well branded. You can learn more about sound-based distinctive brand assets including jingles, audio logos and music tracks in Section 6.6.

Given the contribution that audio elements make to the effectiveness of a video ad, creative teams should spend as much time considering sound design as visual design. The power of music and sound effects should always be leveraged for ads that people will experience with the sound on. Cinema, TV, TikTok and YouTube are predominantly audio-visual. According to research conducted by media attention experts Amplified Intelligence and research company RED C in 2022, some social media channels, however, are mainly visual. The data below was kindly provided to me by Stephen Cleary, Brand Manager for the Irish National Lottery, one of the companies behind the project.

PROPORTION OF AD IMPRESSIONS
THAT HAVE SOUND ON

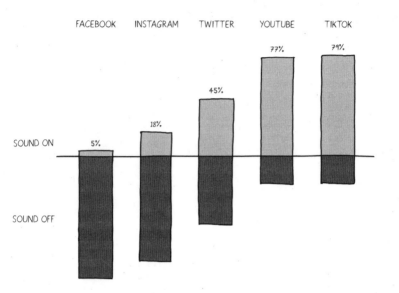

Ads for channels where the sound is usually muted should be optimized for a sound-free experience. Adding subtitles to an ad designed to be seen and heard does little to compensate for the absence of one of our most evocative and influential senses.

8.4 DRAMATIC STRUCTURES

Chuck Young identified four dramatic structures typically used in video advertising in his book *Making Memories*.

DRAMATIC STRUCTURES USED IN ADS

SUSTAINED EMOTION
The ad attempts to sustain a high level of emotional engagement throughout.

EMOTIONAL BUILD
The ad builds emotional engagement gradually to a peak at the end.

POSITIVE SHIFT
The ad starts neutrally but takes emotions to a high level when the brand is introduced.

EMOTIONAL PIVOT
The ad creates increasingly negative emotions which are then reversed when the brand is introduced.

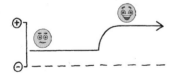
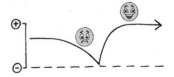

All four structures can be effective. Other dramatic approaches can also work well. If a brand decides to use one of these structures for its advertising, it must understand how to execute it well. It should also know how to interpret market research results in an appropriate way.

SUSTAINED EMOTION

In our world of short and decreasing attention spans, this approach is a good bet. Generating strong, positive emotions right from the start gives the ad a good chance of holding attention before viewers skip or scroll past. To succeed, the ad needs to feel like a fiesta from start to finish. If adopting this approach, introduce the brand at the start and celebrate it being used throughout. Use pace and variety to maintain engagement.

EMOTIONAL BUILD

This dramatic approach starts softly before building to an emotional crescendo. It is potentially the most powerful and memorable approach. It can work well for cinema or TV advertising where the audience is captive, because the slow-build approach has enough time to gather the audience's engagement. In most other media, a gentle start may result in viewers moving past the ad before it has had the chance to work its magic. To make the most of this story-telling structure, ensure the brand comes at the emotional crescendo towards the end, acting as proud 'sponsor' of the underlying idea. This strategy is ideal for brands with a strong purpose.

POSITIVE SHIFT

In positive shift stories, things start being fine, but become a whole lot better when the brand is introduced. This structure only works if viewers realize the brand is responsible for the shift and if the transformation is dramatic enough to stick in the memory. In the modern media environment, it is a risky strategy, better suited to media with longer exposure durations (see Section 8.1).

EMOTIONAL PIVOT

This is a widely used advertising technique also known as Problem-Solution. Everything starts off positively, but then goes horribly wrong until the brand saves the day and makes everything right again. This approach grabs people's attention from the start, then engages them further by introducing a threat, enemy or challenge, before ending on an emotional high. The Emotional Pivot can be very effective because the brand is the hero of the story, coming in when attention is at its highest and having the opportunity to showcase what it can do.

It's worth considering which of these four dramatic structures, if any, your advertising does or could leverage. If none apply, are you sure your adverting will command people's attention? If one applies, will this approach work well given the media you are planning to use? Do your choices make best use of the dramatic potential?

BRANDING FOR VIDEO ADS

Most creative agencies want to produce original, groundbreaking content that wins industry awards. Unfortunately, winning an award does not ensure sales effectiveness. One of the most common shortcomings of advertising is people not registering the brand. Advertising research company Kantar Millward Brown described branding as 'the most variable of variables.' When developing an ad, you need a clear strategy to make sure people can't fail to remember which brand the ad is for.

To consider whether an ad is likely to be well branded, ask yourself and your team this question.

THE SMART BRANDING QUESTION

Does the brand, or one of its distinctive assets, play a lead role in the ad's drama or spectacle?

A good way to test this is to show the ad to a few people who don't work in the industry and ask them to summarize the ad. If they can happily describe it without referring to the brand name, there's a problem with branding that you need to fix.

There are various ways the brand or asset can play a lead role in an ad. The best way depends on the dramatic structure. The four main dramatic structures used in advertising are described in Section 8.4.

DRAMATIC STRUCTURES BRANDING EXAMPLES

SUSTAINED EMOTION

Pringles ads often show people partying with the brand at the centre to the fun.

EMOTIONAL BUILD

Dove's famous ads build to an emotional high, then show the brand's logo and purpose.

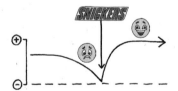

POSITIVE SHIFT

Lipton is known for ads in which everyday moments are made special by drinking the tea.

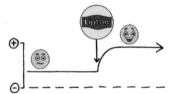

EMOTIONAL PIVOT

Tempers flair because people have become 'hangry' but Snickers makes them normal again.

I have come across one other way an ad can achieve strong brand linkage, without reflecting the best practices described above. Even if an ad is not intrinsically well branded, it can become connected with the brand if it generates high levels of publicity. When this happens, people hear and read about the ad in traditional and social media. The brand name is usually referenced within the articles and posts. When the Cadbury 'Gorilla' ad went viral, people talked about 'that new Cadbury ad with a Gorilla.' You can think of this as 'incentivized' branding, and it is extremely rare.

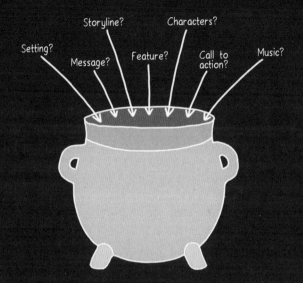

CHAPTER 9

Setting? Storyline? Characters? Music?

Message? Feature? Call to action?

ADVERTISING
RESEARCH

9.1 DEVELOPING YOUR CREATIVE FRAMEWORK

Section 5.2 explored how a marketing team and its creative partners can find a creative framework, or a few alternatives, that might work well for their brand. Market research can be used to help decide which framework has the most potential, but at this stage the team's judgment is equally important. Here are the main factors to consider:

ASSESSING THE POTENTIAL OF CREATIVE PLATFORMS

CONSUMER FEEDBACK CAN HELP ← → NEED TO RELY ON JUDGMENT

| RESONATE EMOTIONALLY | RELEVANT ASSOCIATIONS | A ROLE FOR THE BRAND | DISTINCTIVE ASSETS | GENERATE DISCUSSION | INSPIRE CREATIVITY | FLEXIBLE/ ADAPTABLE |

RESONATE EMOTIONALLY

The best creative platforms resonate strongly with the brand's audience. The development team can't always rely on their intuition about this – for example, if consumers come from a socioeconomic background not represented within the team. It always makes sense to use qualitative research to check whether or not an idea captures the target audience's imagination.

RELEVANT ASSOCIATIONS

The creative platform should lend itself to conjuring associations that are in line with the brand's strategy. A platform based around a teddy bear, for example, lends itself to stories about childhood, comfort and parental love. Consumer feedback can help confirm if the creative idea evokes the kinds of association the brand is aiming for.

A ROLE FOR THE BRAND

As discussed on Section 8.5, advertising often fails because consumers find it hard to connect it with the brand. Ideally, the brand is so central to the idea, that when people describe the advertising, they naturally refer to the brand. This can be checked using qualitative market research.

DISTINCTIVE ASSETS

Featuring well-established assets brings the brand to mind when the advertising is experienced, helping new brand associations to be formed or existing ones to be reinforced. Effective advertising features and strengthens the brand's distinctive assets (see Chapter 6). When choosing a creative platform for your brand, make sure you know how your brand's distinctive assets will be leveraged.

GENERATE DISCUSSION

Occasionally, a brand's advertising is so compelling or socially relevant that it becomes a talking point. This doesn't happen often, but when it does, it can boost the brand's salience for a while.

Predicting whether this will happen is extremely difficult, but there are certain characteristics known to make it more likely (see Section 4.4).

INSPIRE CREATIVITY

A creative platform can only help your brand if it inspires your creative and media partners to produce great work. Market research won't tell you this. You need to sense whether your agency partners are energized by the idea and whether ot not they'll come up with plenty of promising executional ideas.

FLEXIBLE/ADAPTABLE

Creative platforms need to work well in different media, for different advertising tasks (such as brand building and launching new products) and, potentially, across diverse countries and cultures. Market research can be used to inform some of these areas but, ultimately, judgment is required.

Once you have identified your winning creative platform, market research comes into its own. Consumer feedback is invaluable for learning how best to bring the idea to life and make it sing. Creative platforms can be realized for consumers in a variety of ways. The Snickers platform (described in Section 5.1) was initially brought to life through stories featuring famous 'divas,' personifying how people change when they're hungry. More recently, the platform portrayed experts, such as ninjas and spies, who lost their skills and mental focus due to being hungry, before regaining them after eating a Snickers bar. Market research can be used to test storylines that are based on the same underlying creative platform, but feature different scenarios, characters and motivations. This learning helps establish how the overarching idea could be optimized via future executions.

9.2 OPTIMIZING PROTOTYPE ADS

Assuming you have identified a strong creative platform and a promising storyline, the next stage is to create a connected prototype execution. The prototype can be produced in a variety of ways.

- Animatic – drawings or computer-generated images shown in sequence or animated, used to convey the story
- Stealomatic – existing video clips spliced together to tell the story and give an idea of how the final film would look and feel
- Photomatic – a series of still photos, each representing a new scene/moment, used to tell the story
- Rough cut – initial film footage produced for the ad and used to create an early edit
- AI-generated – prototype ad created using an AI platform

You need to decide which of these types of stimuli provides the most accurate impression of how the final ad is intended to look and feel.

Obtaining feedback from the target audience on a prototype of an ad sheds light on its potential.

HOW TO ASSESS A PROTOTYPE AD

Does it grab attention quickly?

Do people find the scenario/characters/ storyline/imagery interesting?

Do people understand what's going on?

Does it hold attention long enough for people to take in what's important?

Does the brand, or one of its assets, play a lead role in the ad's drama or spectacle?

Which elements resonate with the audience? Which fail to be remembered?

What ideas/associations are likely to become connected with the brand?

At this stage, you need to judge whether the final ad, based on this prototype, is likely to be effective. The challenge is that it's often hard to estimate how changes made to the ad, or the final production values, will affect the ad's effectiveness. Minor changes won't usually make much difference, yet there are occasions when they could unlock the ad's potential. The biggest improvements occur when there is an opportunity to make the ad easier to understand, or for the brand's role in the story to be clarified. In my experience, the underlying idea tends to have a bigger influence on an ad's effectiveness than the production. Great ideas shine through even when the execution is mediocre, whereas poor ideas remain ineffective even if they are well-executed.

You can research prototype ads in the following ways:

- Quantitative Pre-testing – this usually involves recruiting a sample of people from the target audience (usually 150-200 respondents), exposing them to the ad and inferring or asking them how it affects their brand perceptions and purchase preferences.
- Qualitative Depth Interviews – individual interviews are preferable to groups for understanding how people respond to advertising, because people mostly experience ads on their own. Group consensus is not relevant and could be misleading.

9.3 ASSESSING FINISHED ADS

If you have already researched your creative platform and proto-type ads, you may not need to assess your final executions. The opportunity for optimization is usually limited at this stage. Testing finished ads is most relevant for marketing teams that choose which ads to use in their region from content produced elsewhere. In this scenario, research can help decide which ads are likely to work best in the local market and obtain insights to optimize them when they are adapted for local use.

The evaluation criteria for prototype ads outlined in Section 9.2 also apply to finished ads. In addition to these dimensions, some brand teams find it useful to have a summary statistic for over-all ad effectiveness, to help them identify the strongest content. Summary metrics usually combine the three factors that relate to in-market effectiveness. Does the ad:

- grab and hold people's attention?
- make people remember which brand is being advertised?
- create brand impressions that people find relevant and motivating?

Brand teams might also find it useful to compare test results with local benchmarks, since this will tell them whether the centrally developed advertising is strong enough to use, or if locally developed content might be a better option.

HOW TO ASSESS A FINISHED AD

Which ad(s) will work best in my country?

Is it as strong as my competitors' current ads?

Are there any opportunities to optimize the ad before we use it?

What can we learn from this, and other projects, to make future ads stronger?

The most relevant benchmarks are:
- Performance of recent ads in your country, used by your brand's closest competitors
- Scores achieved by a cross-section of ads in your country, from a variety of categories

By contrast, historic category norms are generally not relevant. After all, your brand isn't competing with brands from years ago. It is competing with what your competitors are doing today. Also, just because the advertising in your category is generally poor, that doesn't mean you shouldn't set your sights higher. Producing advertising that is significantly better than other brands in the category gives you a significant competitive advantage. I worked in the butter/margarine category in the early 90s. The advertising was universally awful and market shares remained stable. Then, out of nowhere, the brand 'I Can't Believe It's Not Butter' produced exceptional advertising that performed well above all category norms. The brand quickly gained market share. This forced other brands to get their act together. Several competitors improved their advertising and within a couple of years, the category norms had doubled. Historic category norms for creative performance are meaningless.

Finished ads should generally be researched using a quantitative approach. The focus is on predicting in-market effectiveness and less on optimization guidance, so it makes sense to use a fast, low-cost approach even if it is light on diagnostic detail. Using low-cost approaches means you can afford to test your finished advertising as a matter of routine. This enables you to develop general learning to guide future content development. By analysing patterns from 10 or 20 executions, you can start to identify your brand's advertising success formula (see Section 9.5).

9.4 OPTIMIZING YOUR ADVERTISING MIX

You can use various market research techniques to enhance your current and future advertising mix. Early feedback on your current campaign allows you to upweight your strongest ads and optimize your digital media placements before the campaign is over. Post-campaign reviews can identify the media that worked hardest, so you know which channels to prioritize next time.

OPTMIZING YOUR CURRENT MIX OF CREATIVES

It's good practice to use a variety of creatives within each media channel. It increases the chances that everyone in the target audience will respond well to at least one of them, helps to keep the campaign fresh and reduce the effects of diminishing returns (see Section 2.1). However, you may find that certain creatives are much more, or less, effective than others. In this case, in the future it is worth spending more on the strongest ads and less (or nothing) on the weakest. Comparing your creatives is relatively straightforward. A/B testing involves sending a short survey to matched sets of people who have recently been exposed to one or none of the creatives. The survey typically includes measures such as:

- Unaided Brand Awareness
- Purchase Consideration
- Awareness of Brand Communication

The impact of being exposed to each creative can be deduced by comparing the data from the exposed groups with the unexposed group. Some ads have been known to create no uplift at all, whereas others have catapulted the brand to new heights.

For some channels, including linear TV, cinema and print, A/B testing isn't possible because there is no practical way of identifying which individuals have been exposed to each ad. Instead, direct questions about people's reactions to the ads can be used to highlight strong and weak performers.

A typical research project would involve 300-500 category users interviewed a few weeks into the campaign. Research participants are shown various creatives and asked questions to assess:
- Ad recognition
- Enjoyment
- Branding
- Impressions of the brand from the ad
- Persuasiveness

The effectiveness of the ads can be inferred by comparing their scores on these measures. Ad recognition should be treated with caution and only used to compare ads that received the same level of exposure by the time the research took place.

COMPARING THE STRENGTH OF YOUR ADS IN MARKET

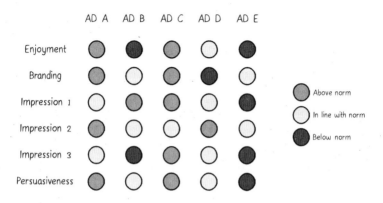

In this example, you might decide to upweight ads A and C, and stop using ad E. Also consider whether your creatives will wear out as you continue using them. However, the evidence from adverting research experts Kantar Millward Brown is clear – creatives do not tend to wear out (Twose, 2019, p147).

If people love an ad the first time they see it, they will love it the tenth time (so long as they don't see it ten times in the same week – see Section 2.1). Similarly, the impressions people get about the brand are almost always the same each time they see the ad. Viewers don't tend to notice more or different things with repeated viewings. The persuasiveness of an ad, however, often declines over time. If the ad initially communicates something new and relevant about the brand, its persuasive effect is strongest during the first few viewings. Subsequent viewings will make people more likely to remember the news, but the ad's newsworthiness and persuasive effect is reduced.

OPTIMIZING YOUR CURRENT MEDIA PLACEMENTS

Advertising campaigns often include different media placements within each digital channel. For example, digital display ads could appear across a wide range of websites and apps. A/B testing can be used to identify which types of websites and apps work best for your campaign. It can also identity which types of people respond most strongly to your campaign – even if it wasn't the people you were anticipating. A/B testing can even establish which creatives work best among different audience profiles. This data can be used to identify which creatives to upweight for the rest of the campaign, which audiences to prioritize, and which websites/apps are best for reaching them.

IMPROVING YOUR NEXT CAMPAIGN'S MEDIA MIX

It's good practice to use a variety of media channels within your advertising mix (see Section 2.4). Combining media that are good at brand-building with media that are good at activating brand memories near the point of purchase is known to be an effective strategy. You can use market research to establish which media channels used in your recent campaign generated the strongest brand-building and activation effects. This data helps you decide which media channels to prioritize in future campaigns. The findings are only relevant, however, if you are planning to use the same or broadly similar creatives in your next campaign. If you are using new creatives, the effectiveness of each channel could be completely different.

This type of research is often called cross media. It usually involves at least 500 interviews conducted over the course of the campaign. The survey includes the same questions used for A/B testing plus additional brand associations:

- Unaided Brand Awareness
- Purchase Consideration
- Brand Associations – a set of dimensions the campaign was intended to strengthen
- Awareness of Brand Communication

In addition, the technique requires data on which elements of the campaign each respondent has been exposed to by the time they were interviewed. This comes from a combination of passive tracking for digital media (respondents' permission having been obtained in advance) and detailed media consumption questions for analogue media. Exposure to the TV ads, for example, is estimated by asking if and when the respondent watches the TV channels or programmes in which the ads are being aired. Ideally, you should also establish how often respondents buy the category because this helps provide an accurate picture of the advertising's immediate sales impact. The analysis involves sophisticated modelling to derive how exposure to different components of the campaign affects the brand measures (especially consideration) and purchasing.

EXAMPLE OUTPUT FROM CROSS MEDIA RESEARCH

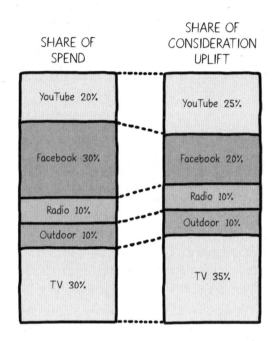

SHARE OF SPEND

SHARE OF CONSIDERATION UPLIFT

YouTube 20%

Facebook 30%

Radio 10%

Outdoor 10%

TV 30%

YouTube 25%

Facebook 20%

Radio 10%

Outdoor 10%

TV 35%

9.5 LEARNING YOUR ADVERTISING SUCCESS FORMULA

One of the advantages of systematically measuring the performance of your advertising is that it provides the opportunity to learn what works and doesn't. Here are four examples.

FOOD BRAND (EUROPE)

Bertolli, known originally as Olivio in the UK, is owned by Unilever. Olivio spread was launched in the UK in 1991 as an alternative to butters and margarines. It is made from olive oil (which was seen as exotic at the time), and the advertising leveraged the fact that people in the Mediterranean live much longer thanks to their diet of fresh fish, vegetables and olive oil. The ads performed well but some were much more impactful and compelling than others. To help enhance the effectiveness of future ads, I conducted an analysis of all the brand's ads up to 1994. It identified some clear success factors. Olivio's most effective ads included several of these features:

- Old people being surprisingly active for their age
- The glorious Mediterranean outdoors
- Varied and delicious-looking fresh produce used to prepare a family meal
- Grandparents interacting with their sons/daughters or, better still, their grandchildren
- The same, distinctive music

These insights helped the team come up with a string of wonderful ads that resonated with consumers, were hugely impactful, and helped accelerate the brand's growth through the 1990s.

OLIVE OIL — AT THE HEART OF A HEALTHY MEDITERRANEAN DIET

TOURISM BRAND (MIDDLE EAST)

The project, conducted in 2021, was for a city in the Middle East aiming to attract tourists and business owners. The city is a fabulous place to live and work. It's clean and safe, full of places to eat and drink, and has lots of interesting things to do and see. The creative team came up with about 40 videos, each featuring a different reason to visit or relocate to the city. By comparing the content of the videos with their ability to get people excited about the city, the most compelling themes and content elements were identified. Here are some of the characteristics that worked best:

- Highlighting an area in which the city leads the world
- Showcasing a unique local attraction

- Featuring an individual explaining why they're happy they moved there
- Hearing from a happy, successful, independent woman

The findings helped the team develop a new series of stories, all of which performed within the top quartile of the initial batch.

VIBRANT MODERN CITY

LUXURY BRAND (GLOBAL)

By looking back at 15 years of advertising, it was possible to identify the most memorable and iconic imagery, moments and themes
from the brand's illustrious back catalogue of ads. By doing this, the
team was able to understand the elements that had become most
strongly associated with the brand and had helped it stand out over
so many years.

Some of the findings were predictable. For example, the brand's strongest ads tended to have a refined setting and feature an elegant woman – ideally someone famous who was renowned for their elegance. Using well-known music also helped.

LUXURY BRAND ADVERTISING IMAGERY

More interestingly, the most powerful ads celebrated the woman and the woman's story. The most memorable imagery captured the woman's strength and dignity. These characteristics were much more important than the fame of the actress. Featuring a strong male character, on the other hand, invariably detracted from the ad's effectiveness.

The analysis showed that subtle sensuality was far more effective than overt sexuality. It also became clear that using a specific colour/visual tone and featuring one of the brand's symbols in a clever way helped people connect the advertising with the right brand. These findings were gold dust.

However, learning from competitors' advertising was even more useful. The advertising produced by two of the brand's closest competitors proved to be far more memorable, and the reason was clear. Each had their own, distinctive tone and style, visual effects, music, sound effects, story structure and symbolism which they had used consistently, across all their advertising, for more than ten years. These observations encouraged the brand owner to define a set of guidelines for future advertising. The guidelines specified which elements from the brand's previous advertising (i.e., the elements found to be most effective and memorable) should be leveraged and evolved in future campaigns.

TOILETRIES BRAND (GLOBAL)

The celebrated 'Campaign for Real Beauty' by the toiletries brand Dove is regarded as one of the world's most effective advertising initiatives. It was the result of a lot of hard thinking and research analysis. I made a small contribution to its development by identifying the success formula of the advertising that came before. Until 2004, Dove used consumer testimonials for most of its ads. They featured an ordinary consumer, always a woman, talking about the product and what she thought about it. The majority worked fairly well but some were vastly superior. The meta-analysis revealed the criteria driving strong performance.

THE WOMAN

How the woman came across in the ad was critical. The more relaxed, natural and genuine the better. This led to lengthy casting sessions to find the perfect person.

THE CONVERSATION

Just talking about the product's functional benefits resulted in advertising that was quickly forgotten. If the testimony also talked about how having good skin made her feel, the ad was more engaging and persuasive.

THE WOMAN'S LIFE

The most effective ads featured women who gave us a glimpse into their lives. If the conversation touched on something other women could identify with, the story helped make the ad more memorable. Everyday topics worked well, such as an anecdote from daily life or how she tried to achieve a good work-life balance.

It became clear that the target audience loved it when they saw a confident, charismatic woman talking in an authentic way about herself and her ordinary life. Further qualitative research confirmed the findings, and this led to the idea of taking female empowerment to the next level in future advertising. The rest, as they say, is history.

DOVE MAINLY USED TESTIMONIALS BEFORE 2004

These examples highlight the benefit of identifying the success formula for your brand's current advertising approach. The key is to collect information on a large set of advertising assets and put them all together in a database that allows you to slice and dice the data with ease. This means that the cost of obtaining the data needs to be low (so you can include lots of assets in the analysis) and the platform needs to be designed with 'general learnings' in mind.

WHAT IS YOUR BRAND'S ADVERTISING SUCCESS FORMULA?

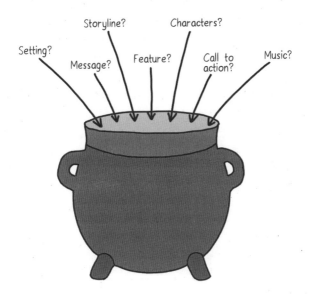

9.6 MEASURING ADVERTISING IMPACT

Measuring the impact of advertising isn't straightforward. Advertising effects can be immediate or span months, years or even decades. Focusing on short-term sales responses can seriously underestimate the value of media investment. The trouble is, you can't measure the long-term effects until they have or haven't happened, by which time it's too late to do anything about it.

This is why savvy marketers look at both short-term sales responses and measures that are indicative of long-term effects, when evaluating the performance of their current advertising. If both short- and long-term indicators are positive, the decision to continue with the current approach is easy. If both indicators are negative, it's clear that stronger advertising must be developed. If the indicators diverge, the business must decide whether to focus on short- or long-term sales.

MEASURING IMMEDIATE IMPACT

The immediate impact of advertising can be measured by comparing daily or weekly ad spend with daily/weekly figures for Key Performance Indicators such as:

- sales revenues
- customer acquisitions
- retail footfall
- website visits
- test drives booked
- search level

The most relevant metric depends on the dynamics of your category (i.e., where/how/when purchases are made) and which measures are known to correlate closely with sales.

ASSESSING LIKELY LONG-TERM SALES IMPACT

The likely long-term sales impact of advertising can be assessed before it has happened by measuring how the advertising affects brand metrics that generally relate to long-term sales. Communications Awareness, Unaided Brand Awareness and Purchase Consideration are usually the best options. These metrics can be obtained via brand surveys conducted either continuously or just before and towards the end of a stretch of advertising. Samples sizes of 300-500 per dip or 30-50 per week are typical.

HOW BRAND MEASURES
RESPOND TO GOOD ADVERTISING

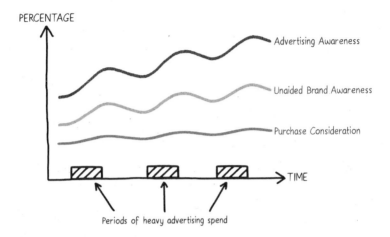

Periods of heavy advertising spend

If your advertising is strong, you can expect to see a good uplift in Advertising Awareness – assuming there has been little or no advertising in the previous three months. The uplift to expect from each burst depends on the pre-burst level and the amount of spend. It can vary from five to ten percentage points for established brands and more for new brands. You should also see a clear response in Unaided Brand Awareness, although the uplifts will be smaller. Purchase Consideration should also increase, but to an extent that will normally be too small to measure accurately in the short term given the statistical sample error associated with surveys with a few hundred respondents. Purchase Consideration is also heavily influenced by what competitors are doing, and its impact should be reviewed over the longer term. Assuming your product, price and availability are competitive, you should see a gradual rise resulting from the cumulative impact over several waves of advertising. Continuous weekly data can be aggregated into rolling 16- or 24-week blocks to make tracking easier.

TARGET SETTING

You can assess whether your brand is progressing as required by setting targets based on your commercial objectives. For example, if your goal is to increase market share from 20% to 25% from one year to the next, you should aim for Share of Brand Consideration to increase by the same ratio. If Share of Brand Consideration is 23% in Year One, it needs to reach 29% (23% X 25%/20%) in Year Two.

Most measures on a typical brand survey change slowly over the long term, even if they rise and fall in the shorter term. This is because the overall saliency of the brand fluctuates. Many brand attributes move slowly because people only use them to describe a brand in a survey if they have experienced the brand first-hand. These types of measure tend to move in line with purchasing (provided the product lives up to the expectations created by the advertising, of course):

- Brand I prefer
- High quality
- Meets my needs
- Trustworthy
- Easy to use
- Exciting to drive
- Good for dry skin
- Creamy taste
- Highly refreshing
- Good customer service
- Etc.

It is possible, however, for advertising to reshape how people think about your brand and to build strong associations with specific ideas and usage contexts (see Section 1.3). The illustration below shows what you need to look for to determine if your brand's image is heading in the right direction. All brand dimensions tend to move together (in line with fluctuations in the brand's overall saliency), but you should see target dimensions start to move ahead of the pack if your advertising is having the desired effect.

HOW BRAND ASSOCIATIONS EVOLVE OVER TIME

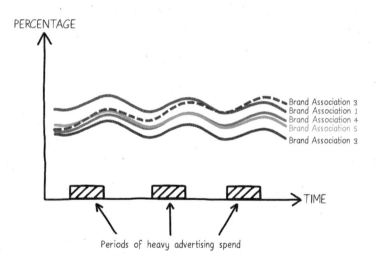

Periods of heavy advertising spend

It is worth noting that certain types of brand association can respond quickly to advertising. If a campaign communicates a fact or claim about the brand in a credible and compelling way, the uplift can be almost as large as the uplift in Communications Awareness. I have seen very large increases in dimensions akin to the ones below:

- Now open 24/7
- 10-year, money-back guarantee
- Recommended by doctors
- Made from Cornish clotted cream
- Most popular brand in Australia
- Competitive prices
- The make-up used by make-up artists (when this claim was new)

EVALUATING ADVERTISING WITH CONTINUOUS SPEND

So far in this section, it has been assumed that a brand's advertising spend varies over time and has periods of light and heavy activity. This makes it possible to quantify the effects of advertising by measuring the uplifts associated with higher spend levels. However, leading brands in high value categories are likely to spend heavily on a near-continuous basis. This makes it more difficult to isolate and evaluate the advertising contribution.

THE IMPACT OF CONTINUOUS ADVERTISING

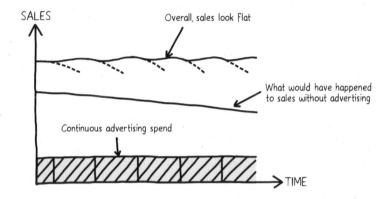

Brands in this situation cannot use pre-post shift to assess the impact of their advertising. Instead, they need to rely on other research methods:

- Copy-testing to assess likely short- and long-term sales effects
- Cross Media research to estimate the effects of a burst of advertising
- Comparing data between regions with different levels of spend
- Sales modelling to compare advertising spend with its contribution to sales and profit (over a period of at least two years)

CONCLUSION

Advertising development is possibly the most fascinating, rewarding, frustrating and difficult challenge a marketer will face. The stakes are high because the cost of developing, producing and deploying advertising can be huge, whereas the return on this investment is wildly variable. Having read *The Smart Advertising Book*, you should have enough knowledge about the practicalities and science of advertising development to give you the best possible chance of success.

Advertising is one of the best investments a brand could make – but only if you take the long-term view. Industry practice does not currently reflect this. Be strong when challenged about investing in brand-building advertising (Section 1.5). It may be right for the business, but not everyone will see it the same way.

CONVERSATION BETWEEN CFO AND CMO

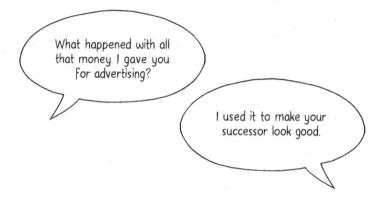

I wish you the best of luck. Please let me know how it goes and what you've learned that might help the next generation of marketers do an even better job (dan.j.white@me.com).

BIBLIOGRAPHY

Binet, Les, and Field, Peter. *The Long and the Short of It: Balancing Short and Long-Term Marketing Strategies*. London: Institute of Practitioners in Advertising, 2013.

Chaffey, Dave. '2023 Average Ad Click Through Rates (CTRs) for Paid Search, Display and Social Media.' *SmartInsights.com*, 14 February, 2023. https://www.smartinsights.com/internet-advertising/internet-advertising-analytics/display-advertising-clickthrough-rates/.

'Unlocking the New Economy of Attention.' *Dentsu.com*. Last modified 12 May, 2021. https://www.dentsu.com/uk/en/our-latest-thinking/unlocking-the-new-currency-of-attention).

'The Challenge of Attention.' *Ebiquity.com*. Last modified September, 2022. https://www.ebiquity.com/news-insights/viewpoints/the-challenge-of-attention.

Eisend, Martin. 'A Meta-analysis of Humor in Advertising.' *Journal of the Academy of Marketing Science* 37 no. 2 (2009): 191–203. https://link.springer.com/article/10.1007/s11747-008-0096-y.

Fisman, Ray. 'Did eBay Just Prove That Paid Search Ads Don't Work?' *Harvard Business Review*, 11 March, 2013. https://hbr.org/2013/03/did-ebay-just-prove-that-paid.

Gijsenberg, Maarten and Nijs, Vincent. 'Advertising Spending Patterns and Competitor Impact.' *International Journal of Research in Marketing* 36 no. 2 (June 2019): 232-250. https://doi.org/10.1016/j.ijresmar.2018.11.004.

Hankins, James. 'The Hankins Hexagon: A New Practical Model for the Path to Purchase.' *WARC*, 2021. https://www.warc.com/content/paywall/article/warc-exclusive/the-hankins-hexagon-a-new-practical-model-for-the-path-to-purchase/en-gb/137888.

Hiwaizi, Omaid. 'Forget About X, Y and Z: Welcome to Generation Curious.' *Campaign Magazine*, 9 July, 2015. https://www.campaignlive.co.uk/article/forget-x-y-z-welcome-generation-curious/1355380?src_site=marketingmagazine.

'Millward Brown Knowledge Point – Can I Make My Ad Go Viral?' *IABAustralia.com.au*. Last modified 2011. https://iabaustralia.com.au/wp-content/uploads/2011/09/Millward-Brown-Can-I-make-my-Ad-go-Viral.pdf.

Ivana V. 'Direct Mail Statistics That Will Have You Running to the Post Office.' *Smallbizgenius.net*, 17 June, 2023. https://www.smallbizgenius.net/by-the-numbers/direct-mail-statistics/#gref).

'The Art of Proof: How Creative Quality Drives Profit.' *Kantar.com*. Last modified 9 February, 2023. https://www.kantar.com/inspiration/advertising-media/the-art-of-proof-how-creative-quality-drives-profit.

'Who's Laughing Now? Let's Stop the Decline of Humour in Advertising.' *Kantar.com*. Last modified 3 February, 2022. https://www.kantar.com/inspiration/advertising-media/how-to-get-humour-right-in-advertising).

'Product Demos in Advertising; How to Get Them Right.' *Kantar.com*. Last modified 12 July, 2022. https://www.kantar.com/north-america/inspiration/advertising-media/product-demos-in-advertising-how-to-get-them-right.

Kim, Soojin and Kim, Jihye. 'The Effect of Visual Metaphor in Advertising.' *Visual Communications* Journal 55 no. 2 (August 2019): 16-31. https://www.researchgate.net/publication/335651132_The_effect_of_visual_metaphor_in_advertising.

Kite, Grace. 'Three Data Led Pointers for Budget Season.' *Magicnumbers.co.uk*. Last modified March 2023. https://magicnumbers.co.uk/articles/three-data-led-pointers-for-budget-season/.

Luca, Michael. 'Reviews, Reputation, and Revenue: The Case of Yelp.com.' *Harvard Business School Working Paper*, No. 12-016, September 2016. https://www.hbs.edu/faculty/Pages/item.aspx?num=41233#:~:text=I%20present%20three%20findings%20about,and%20(3)%20chain%20Orestaurants%20have.

'Email Marketing Statistics and Benchmarks by Industry.' *Mailchimp.com*. Last modified 29 July, 2019. https://mailchimp.com/resources/email-marketing-benchmarks/.

Marchant, Ross. 'What Star Rating is Too Low for a Local Business?' 12 August, 2014. https://www.brightlocal.com/blog/average-star-rating-low-consider-using-local-business/

'Mentos Viral Marketing Case Study.' *Marketingandmichael.wordpress.com*. Last modified 10 July, 2015. https://marketingandmichael.wordpress.com/2015/07/10/mentos-viral-marketing-case-study/.

'The 95:5 Rule Is the New 60:40 Rule.' *Marketingscience.info*. Last modified 2 September, 2021. https://www.marketingscience.info/the-955-rule-is-the-new-6040-rule/.

McQuarrie, Edward and Mick, David. 'Visual and Verbal Rhetorical Figures under Directed Processing versus Incidental Exposure to Advertising.' *Journal of Consumer Research* 29 no. 4 (March 2003): 579–587. https://academic.oup.com/jcr/article-abstract/29/4/579/1791064.

McQuarrie, Edward and Phillips, Barbara. 'Indirect Persuasion in Advertising: How Consumers Process Metaphors Presented in Pictures and Words.' *Journal of Advertising* 34 no. 2 (March 2013): 7-20. https://www.researchgate.net/publication/261662288_Indirect_persuasion_in_advertising_How_consumers_process_metaphors_presented_in_pictures_and_words.

Nielsen.com. 'When it Comes to Advertising Effectiveness, What is Key?' Last modified October 2017. https://www.nielsen.com/insights/2017/when-it-comes-to-advertising-effectiveness-what-is-key/.

Phillips, Barbara. 'Understanding Visual Metaphor in Advertising,' in Scott, Linda and Batra, Rajeev. *Persuasive Imagery: A Consumer Response Perspective*. Abingdon-on-Thames: Routledge, 2003.

Quesenberry, Keith and Coolsen, Michael. 'What Makes a Super Bowl Ad Super? Five-Act Dramatic Form Affects Consumer Super Bowl Advertising Ratings.' *The Journal of Marketing Theory and Practice* 22 No. 4 (October 2014): 437-454. https://researchgate.net/publication/273336153_What_Makes_a_Super_Bowl_Ad_Super_Five-Act_Dramatic_Form_Affects_Consumer_Super_Bowl_Advertising_Ratings.

Sharp, Byron. *How Brands Grow*. Melbourne: Oxford University Press, 2010.

Sliburyte, Laimona. 'How Celebrities Can Be Used in Advertising to the Best Advantage?' International Journal of Social, Behavioural, Educational, Business and Industrial Engineering 3 no. 10 (October 2009). https://www.researchgate.net/publication/283797394_How_celebrities_can_be_used_in_advertising_to_the_best_advantage.

Snyder, Jasper and Garcia-Garcia, Manuel. 'Advertising across Platforms: Conditions for Multimedia Campaigns – A Method for Determining Optimal Media Investment and Creative Strategies across Platforms.' *Journal of Advertising Research* 42 (December 2016). https://www.journalofadvertisingresearch.com/content/56/4/352.figures-only.

'How Online Reviews Influence Sales.' *Spiegel.medill.northwestern.edu*. Last modified June 2017. https://spiegel.medill.northwestern.edu/wp-content/uploads/sites/2/2021/04/Spiegel_Online-Review_eBook_Jun2017_FINAL.pdf.

Twose, Dominic. *Marketing Knowledge*. Morrisville: Lulu.com, 2019.

Young, Chuck. *Making Memories*. Seattle: Ideas in Flight, 2020.

'Making a Lasting Impression – Kantar Millward Brown.' *YouTube.com*. Last modified 2017. https://www.youtube.com/watch?v=gDhr5BB7wuE.

Zatwarnicka-Madura, Beata and Nowacki, Robert. 'Storytelling and its Impact on Effectiveness of Advertising.' *8th International Conference on Management – Leadership, Innovativeness and Entrepreneurship in a Sustainable Economy* (November 2018). https://www.researchgate.net/publication/329035582_STORYTELLING_AND_ITS_IMPACT_ON_EFFECTIVENESS_OF_ADVERTISING.

Zhang, Hantian. 'Prime: A YouTuber Expert Explains How Logan Paul and KSI's Drink Became so Popular.' *The Conversation*. Last modified 17 March, 2023. https://theconversation.com/prime-a-youtuber-expert-explains-how-logan-paul-and-ksis-drink-became-so-popular-201792#:~:text=Through%20their%20audience%20engagement%20strategies,created%20a%20hugely%20popular%20brand.

Znanewitz, Judith and Gilch, Kim. 'Storytelling – A guideline and an application in the Bundeswehr's (personnel) marketing.' *Transfer, Werbeforschung & Praxis: Zeitschrift für Werbung, Kommunikation und Markenführung* Volume 4 (December 2016): 30-35. https://www.econbiz.de/Record/storytelling-a-guideline-and-an-application-in-the-bundeswehr-s-personnel-marketing-hattke-judith/10011581754.

ACKNOWLEDGEMENTS

I have many people to thank for making this book possible.

My son, Alex, has devoted many days to making sure everything in the book looks and sounds good, is based on fact not hearsay, and makes sense to everyone. It has been fun to work with him.

I also want to thank the many people who have contributed their thoughts, examples and anecdotes on my LinkedIn posts. Thank you for being a sounding board and source of inspiration. I hope you can all see how your ideas have shaped the content. The list below is far from comprehensive, so I apologise if I have not included your name:

Gabriel Agüero, Ryan Barry, Les Binet, Marc Binkley, Jon Bradshaw, Johnny Corbett, Vassilis Douros, Paul Dyson, Tom Elmer, Jon Evans, Paul Feldwick, John Fix, Mike Follett, James Hankins, Nigel Hollis, Matthias Höppner, Nicolas Huber, Brian Jacobs, Grace Kite, Jim Knapp, Adrian Langford, Paul Lewis, Julian Major, Kim Malcolm, Steve Messenger, Ian Murray, Andrew Mushing, Philip Oakley, Koen Pauwels, Leo Pérez, Jason Quehl, Tom Roach, AJ Rollsy, Jenni Roma- niuk, Byron Sharp, Tim Sparke, Graham Staplehurst, Ian Thompson, Bert Valk, Nicholas Vechi, Gareth Walters, Craig Ward, Karl Weaver, Mark Wieczorek, Orlando Wood, Chuck Young.

ABOUT THE AUTHOR

DAN WHITE is a marketing and insights innovator. His career includes a decade as an insights professional, another as a brand advisor and a third as a Chief Marketing Officer.

Dan co-developed BRANDZ, the world's biggest brand equity measurement system and his thinking has shaped the design of leading copy test and brand tracking methodologies. As a brand and communications guru, he has advised famous, billion-dollar brands on how to thrive and his summaries and trademark visualizations have earned praise from luminaries in the marketing, advertising and media industries.

Every sentence and every hand-drawn illustration in *The Smart Advertising Book* has been crafted to ensure readers can understand and apply the often-complex concepts needed to make smart advertising choices.

FROM THE SAME AUTHOR

The Smart Marketing Book
LID Publishing, 2020

£12.99/$14.95
ISBN: 978-1-912555-76-5

The Soft Skills Book
LID Publishing, 2021

£12.99/$14.95
ISBN: 978-1-911671-54-1

The Smart Branding Book
LID Publishing, 2022

£9.99/$12.95
ISBN: 978-1-911687-70-2